First World War
and Army of Occupation
War Diary
France, Belgium and Germany

2 DIVISION
19 Infantry Brigade
Princess Louise's (Argyll & Sutherland Highlanders)
2nd Battalion
2 February 1914 - 30 November 1915

WO95/1365/1

The Naval & Military Press Ltd
www.nmarchive.com
Published in association with The National Archives

Published by

The Naval & Military Press Ltd

Unit 10 Ridgewood Industrial Park,

Uckfield, East Sussex,

TN22 5QE England

Tel: +44 (0) 1825 749494

www.naval-military-press.com

www.nmarchive.com

This diary has been reprinted in facsimile from the original. Any imperfections are inevitably reproduced and the quality may fall short of modern type and cartographic standards.

© **Crown Copyright**

Images reproduced by permission of The National Archives, London, England, 2015.

Contents

Document type	Place/Title	Date From	Date To
Heading	WO95/1365/1		
Heading	2 Division 33 Bde 2 Bn A & S Highland 1914 Aug-1915 Nov To 33 Div		
Heading	19th Infantry Brigade 2nd Battalion Argyll & Sutherland Highlanders August 1914		
War Diary		05/08/1917	31/08/1917
Heading	19th Infantry Brigade. 2nd Battalion Argyll & Sutherland Highlanders September 1914		
War Diary	Salines	01/09/1914	01/09/1914
War Diary	Nery	01/09/1914	01/09/1914
War Diary	Fresnoy	01/09/1914	02/09/1914
War Diary	Baron	02/09/1914	02/09/1914
War Diary	Eve	02/09/1914	02/09/1914
War Diary	Longperrier	02/09/1914	03/09/1914
War Diary	Lagny	03/09/1914	05/09/1914
War Diary	Grissy	05/09/1914	06/09/1914
War Diary	Ozoir La Ferriere	06/09/1914	07/09/1914
War Diary	La Haute Maison	07/09/1914	08/09/1914
War Diary	Signy	08/09/1914	08/09/1914
War Diary	Ch. Venteuil	08/09/1914	09/09/1914
War Diary	Signy	09/09/1914	09/09/1914
War Diary	Jouarre	09/09/1914	10/09/1914
War Diary	Marcy Fm	10/09/1914	10/09/1914
War Diary	Certigny	10/09/1914	10/09/1914
War Diary	Passy En Valois	11/09/1914	11/09/1914
War Diary	Maritzy-St-Genevieve	11/09/1914	12/09/1914
War Diary	Buzancy	12/09/1914	13/09/1914
War Diary	Septmonts	13/09/1914	14/09/1914
War Diary	Venizel	14/09/1914	16/09/1914
War Diary	Bucy-Le-Long	17/09/1914	17/09/1914
War Diary	La Marguerite	17/09/1914	17/09/1914
War Diary	Bucy-Le-Long	17/09/1914	21/09/1914
War Diary	Venizel	21/09/1914	21/09/1914
War Diary	Septmonts	22/09/1914	30/09/1914
War Diary	Crepy-En-Valois	01/09/1914	01/09/1914
War Diary	Nanteuil	02/09/1914	02/09/1914
Miscellaneous	Montyon	03/09/1914	03/09/1914
War Diary	Villiers S/Morin	04/09/1914	04/09/1914
War Diary	Jossigny	05/09/1914	05/09/1914
War Diary	Grissy	05/09/1914	05/09/1914
War Diary	Le Mans	01/09/1914	04/09/1914
War Diary	Grissy	05/09/1914	05/09/1914
Heading	19th Infantry Brigade. 2nd Battalion Argyll & Sutherland Highlanders (October 1914)		
Heading	War Diary of 2nd Battalion Argylle & Sutherland Highlanders 19th Brigade From 1st October 1914 To 31st October 1914 (Volume 3.)		
Miscellaneous	Index		
War Diary	Septmonts	01/10/1914	05/10/1914
War Diary	St Remy	06/10/1914	06/10/1914

War Diary	Vez	07/10/1917	07/10/1917
War Diary	Bethisy St-Pierre	07/10/1917	08/10/1917
War Diary	Pont-St-Maxence	08/10/1917	09/10/1917
War Diary	Estrees-St-Benis	09/10/1914	10/10/1914
War Diary	Blendecques	10/10/1914	10/10/1914
War Diary	St Omer	10/10/1914	10/10/1914
War Diary	Watten	10/10/1914	10/10/1914
War Diary	St Omer	10/10/1914	11/10/1914
War Diary	Fort Rouge	11/10/1914	11/10/1914
War Diary	Renescure	11/10/1914	12/10/1914
War Diary	Les Cinq Rues	12/10/1914	12/10/1914
War Diary	La Kreule	12/10/1914	12/10/1914
War Diary	Eecke	12/10/1914	13/10/1914
War Diary	Rouge Croix	13/10/1914	14/10/1914
War Diary	Le Leuthe Fe	14/10/1914	14/10/1914
War Diary	Mont Lille	14/10/1914	15/10/1914
War Diary	Bailleul	15/10/1914	15/10/1914
War Diary	Steenwerk	15/10/1914	16/10/1914
War Diary	Neuve-Eglise	16/10/1914	16/10/1914
War Diary	Vlamertinghe	16/10/1917	16/10/1917
War Diary	Laventie	20/10/1914	20/10/1914
War Diary	Fromelles	20/10/1914	21/10/1914
War Diary	Le Maisnil	21/10/1914	21/10/1914
War Diary	Bas Maisnil	21/10/1914	21/10/1914
War Diary	La Boutillerie	21/10/1914	29/10/1914
Miscellaneous	A Form Messages And Signals		
Map	Le Maisnil		
Miscellaneous			
Heading	19th Infantry Brigade. 2nd Battalion Argyle & Sutherland Highlanders November 1914.		
Heading	War Diary of 2nd Bn Argyll & Sutherland Highlanders 19th Brigade From 1st November 1914 To 30th November 1914 (Volume IV)		
Miscellaneous	Table Of Contents		
War Diary	Farm between La Boutillerie and Le Touquet	01/11/1914	01/11/1914
War Diary	Erquinghem	02/11/1914	02/11/1914
War Diary	Pont De Nieppe	02/11/1914	07/11/1914
War Diary	Le Bizet	07/11/1914	07/11/1914
War Diary	Ploegsteert	07/11/1914	07/11/1914
War Diary	Touquet	07/11/1914	07/11/1914
War Diary	Ploegsteert	07/11/1914	07/11/1914
War Diary	Touquet	07/11/1914	07/11/1914
War Diary	Ploegsteert	07/11/1914	08/11/1914
War Diary	Ploegsteert Wood	09/11/1914	13/11/1914
War Diary	Mill Ploegsteert	13/11/1914	13/11/1914
War Diary	Rue Bataille	13/11/1914	17/11/1914
War Diary	Houplines	17/11/1914	30/11/1914
Miscellaneous	A Form Messages And Signals		
Map	Appendix B		
Miscellaneous	C Form Messages And Signals		
Heading	19th Infantry Brigade. 2 Div 1365 2nd Battalion Argyle & Sutherland Highlanders December 1914.		
Heading	War Diary of 19th Brigade 2nd Battalion, Argyll & Sutherland Highlanders From 1st December 1914 To 31st December 1914 (Volume 5)		
Miscellaneous	Index		

War Diary	Houplines	01/12/1914	11/12/1914
War Diary	Lunatic Asylum Armentieres	11/12/1914	20/12/1914
War Diary	Houplines (Trenches)	20/12/1914	26/12/1914
War Diary	Houplines	26/12/1914	26/12/1914
War Diary	Armentieres	26/12/1914	31/12/1914
Miscellaneous	Special 6th Division Operation Order No.	01/12/1914	01/12/1914
Miscellaneous	19th Infantry Brigade	09/12/1914	09/12/1914
War Diary	Armentieres	01/01/1915	02/01/1915
War Diary	Bois Grenier (Trenches)	02/01/1915	13/01/1915
War Diary	Gris Pot	14/01/1915	18/01/1915
War Diary	La Vesee (trenches)	18/01/1915	23/01/1915
War Diary	L'Armee	23/01/1915	28/01/1915
War Diary	La Vesee (trenches)	29/01/1915	31/01/1915
Heading	War Diary 2nd Battn. The Argyll & Sutherland Highlanders February 1915		
War Diary	Nr Bois Grenier	01/02/1915	02/02/1915
War Diary	L'Armee	02/02/1914	06/02/1914
War Diary	Nr Bois Grenier	07/02/1915	12/02/1915
War Diary	L'Armee	12/02/1915	17/02/1915
War Diary	Nr Bois Grenier	17/02/1915	18/02/1915
War Diary	Bois Grenier	19/02/1915	22/02/1915
War Diary	L'Armee	22/02/1915	27/02/1915
War Diary	Nr Bois Grenier	27/02/1915	28/02/1915
Heading	War Diary 2nd Battn. The Argyll & Sutherland Highlanders. March 1915		
War Diary	Nr Bois Grenier	01/03/1915	04/03/1915
War Diary	L'Armee	04/03/1915	09/03/1915
War Diary	Nr Bois Grenier	09/03/1915	15/03/1915
War Diary	L'Armee	15/03/1915	31/03/1915
Heading	War Diary 2nd Battn. The Argyll & Sutherland Highlanders. April 1915		
War Diary	Nr Bois Grenier	01/04/1915	04/04/1915
War Diary	Gris Pot	05/04/1915	08/04/1915
War Diary	Rue De Bois	08/04/1915	12/04/1915
War Diary	Gris Pot	13/04/1915	18/04/1915
War Diary	Rue De Bois	18/04/1915	23/04/1915
War Diary	Grispot	24/04/1915	27/04/1915
War Diary	Rue De Bois	28/04/1915	30/04/1915
Heading	19th Inf Bde 5th Div War Diary 2nd Battn. The Argyll & Sutherland Highlanders. May 1915		
War Diary	Rue De Bois	01/05/1915	03/05/1915
War Diary	Gris Pot	04/05/1915	08/05/1915
War Diary	Rue De Bois	09/05/1915	13/05/1915
War Diary	Gris Pot	14/05/1915	18/05/1915
War Diary	Rue Du Bois	19/05/1917	23/05/1917
War Diary	Gris Pot	24/05/1915	28/05/1915
War Diary	Rue Du Bois	28/05/1915	31/05/1915
Heading	27th Division 19th Infy Bde 2nd Bn A. & S HDRS Jun-Jul 1915		
Heading	19th Infantry Brigade. 27th Division. 2nd Battn. The Argyll And Sutherland Highlanders		
Heading	War Diary of 2nd Battalion Argyll & Sutherland Highlanders From 1st June 1915 To 30th June 1915 Vol XI		
Miscellaneous	Index		
War Diary	Rue Du Bois	01/06/1915	02/06/1915

War Diary	Gus Pot	03/06/1915	04/06/1915
War Diary	Bois Grenier	05/06/1915	10/06/1915
War Diary	Gus Pot	11/06/1915	12/06/1915
War Diary	Rue Du Bois	13/06/1915	18/06/1915
War Diary	Gris Pot	19/06/1915	20/06/1915
War Diary	Nr. Rue du Bois	21/06/1915	23/06/1915
War Diary	Rue Du Bois	24/06/1915	27/06/1915
War Diary	Gris Pot	28/06/1915	30/06/1915
Miscellaneous	Appendices		
Miscellaneous	Farewell Message to 19th Infantry Brigade.	13/06/1915	13/06/1915
Miscellaneous	A Form Messages And Signals		
Miscellaneous	Report On Reconnaissance Carried Out On The Night	21/06/1915	21/06/1915
Heading	19th Infantry Brigade. 27th Division. 2nd Battn. The Argyll And Sutherland Highlanders. July 1915		
Heading	War Diary 2nd Battalion Argyll South High From 1st July 1915 To 31st July 1915		
War Diary	Gris Pot	01/07/1915	01/07/1915
War Diary	Nr Rue Du Bois	02/07/1915	06/07/1915
War Diary	Gris Pot	07/07/1915	11/07/1915
War Diary	Nr. Rue du Bois	12/07/1915	16/07/1915
War Diary	La Rolan Devil Farm	17/07/1915	19/07/1915
War Diary	Erquinghem Road Function	19/07/1915	19/07/1915
War Diary	Nr.Pt. Mortar	20/07/1915	23/07/1915
War Diary	Pincantin Post	23/07/1915	29/07/1915
War Diary	Nouveau-Monde	30/07/1915	31/07/1915
Miscellaneous	Appendices		
Miscellaneous	Officer Commanding	17/07/1915	17/07/1915
Operation(al) Order(s)	19th Infantry Brigade Operation Order No:42	18/07/1915	18/07/1915
Miscellaneous	B.M./0.3	18/07/1915	18/07/1915
Miscellaneous	Issued with Operation Order No:42.		
Miscellaneous	Speech of Lieutenant General Sir W.P. Pulteney, K.C.B. D.S.O. Commanding 3rd Corps		
Miscellaneous	Warning Order	21/07/1915	21/07/1915
Operation(al) Order(s)	19th Infantry Brigade Operation Order No:43	22/07/1915	22/07/1915
Miscellaneous	19th Infantry Brigade After Order To Be Attached To Operation Order No. 43	22/07/1915	22/07/1915
Miscellaneous	March Table Battalions 19th Infantry Brigade	23/07/1915	23/07/1915
Miscellaneous	Battalion Orders By Lieutenant-Colonel, R.C. Gore	22/07/1915	22/07/1915
Heading	2nd Division 19th Infy Bde 2nd Battalion Argyll & Sutherland Hdrs. Aug-Nov 1915. To 33 Div 98 Bde		
Heading	War Diary 19th Infantry Brigade. 2nd Division 2nd Battn. The Argyll & Sutherland Highlanders August 1915		
Heading	War Diary. 2nd. Battalion, Argyll & Sutherland Highlanders. From 1st. August, 1915 To 31st August, 1915.		
War Diary	Nouveau Monde	01/08/1915	04/08/1915
War Diary	Laventie	05/08/1915	06/08/1915
War Diary	Picantin	07/08/1915	08/08/1915
War Diary	(Picantin) Picantin	09/08/1915	16/08/1915
War Diary	Vieux Berquin	17/08/1915	19/08/1915
War Diary	Bethune	20/08/1915	24/08/1915
War Diary	Orchard Redoubt	25/08/1915	28/08/1915
War Diary	Beuvry	29/08/1915	31/08/1915
Miscellaneous	Appendices		
Miscellaneous	Appendix. A1.	15/08/1915	15/08/1915

Operation(al) Order(s)	19th Infantry Brigade Operation Order No.44	14/08/1915	14/08/1915
Miscellaneous	3rd Corps.	14/08/1915	14/08/1915
Operation(al) Order(s)	March Order No:45	18/08/1915	18/08/1915
Miscellaneous	March Table-19th Infantry Brigade	19/08/1915	19/08/1915
Miscellaneous	Officer Commanding	21/08/1915	21/08/1915
Operation(al) Order(s)	19th Infantry Brigade Operation Order No:43	23/08/1915	23/08/1915
Miscellaneous	March Table, 19th Infantry Brigade.		
Heading	19th Infantry Brigade. 2nd Division. War Diary 2nd Battn. The Argyll And Sutherland Highlanders. September 1915		
Heading	War Diary of 2nd Battalion Argyll & Sutherland High From 1st 11 September 1915 To 30th September 1915		
War Diary	Beuvry	01/09/1915	01/09/1915
War Diary	Nr Cambrin	01/09/1915	04/09/1915
War Diary	Bethune	05/09/1915	05/09/1915
War Diary	Essars	06/09/1915	13/09/1915
War Diary	Nr Le Preol	13/09/1915	17/09/1915
War Diary	Nr Cambrin	17/09/1915	20/09/1915
War Diary	Nr Bethune	20/09/1915	23/09/1915
War Diary	Cambrin	24/09/1915	27/09/1915
War Diary	Annequin	28/09/1915	30/09/1915
Heading	19th Infantry Brigade. 2nd Division 2nd Battn. The Argyll & Sutherland Highlanders October 1915		
Heading	War Diary of 2nd Bn Arg South Highlanders From 1st October 1915 To 31st October 1915		
War Diary	Cambrin	01/10/1915	01/10/1915
War Diary	Nr Anneqin	02/10/1915	02/10/1915
War Diary	Bethune	04/10/1915	16/10/1915
War Diary	Cambrin	17/10/1915	20/10/1915
War Diary	Annequin	20/10/1915	25/10/1915
War Diary	Cambrin	25/10/1915	30/10/1915
War Diary	Gonnehem	31/10/1915	31/10/1915
Heading	19th Infantry Brigade 2nd Division 2nd Battn. The Argyll & Sutherland Highlanders November 1915		
War Diary	Gonnehem	01/11/1915	07/11/1915
War Diary	Route	07/11/1915	07/11/1915
War Diary	Beuvry	08/11/1915	12/11/1915
War Diary	Anniquin	12/11/1915	18/11/1915
War Diary	Cambrin	18/11/1915	23/11/1915
War Diary	Bethune	23/11/1915	24/11/1915
War Diary	Mt Berenchon	24/11/1915	30/11/1915
War Diary	Le Touret	30/11/1915	30/11/1915
Miscellaneous	Appendix "A"		
Miscellaneous	Report On Operations On Monday	22/11/1915	22/11/1915
Miscellaneous	7 Div		

W0005/13965/1

2 DIVISION

33 BDE

2 BN A & S HIGHLANDERS

1914 AUG — 1915 NOV

TO 33 DIV.

19th Infantry Brigade

2nd BATTALION

ARGYLE & SUTHERLAND HIGHLANDERS

AUGUST 1914.

WAR DIARY.

August 5th Wednesday — 5.30 pm. Received the order "MOBILIZE". proceeded according to Mobilization Tables

Thursday 6th — 3 pm. Completed Mobilization to Peace Strength. Took over 91 Prisoners of War (Germans, Dutch, and Austrians) taken from a fishing fleet sunk in the NORTH SEA by H.M.S.

The prisoners were confined in the moat by day and in 3 Casemates by night. All very cheery.

Friday 7th — 4 am. 1st Party of Reservists under Capt. Thomson 2/Lieuts Connal-Rowan Colquhoun & Fairlie arrived, strength 400.

2.30 pm. Received orders "Embark Expeditionary Force, taking 9th August as 1st day of Movement.

Saturday 8th — 4 am. 2nd Party of Reservists arrived under Capt. Muir, Lieut Connal-Rowan, & 2/Lieut Buchanan strength 300. Lieut Bennet (from Colonial Force) and 2/Lieut Anderson also joined.

1 pm. Order received to move Battalion to SOUTHAMPTON on 9th August in 4 parties, the 1st leaving at 6.10 pm.

Mobilization completed, but no time available for exercising Remounts in wagons as fitting of harness took every minute. Contrary orders received regarding carrying of spare shoes in Base kit caused great trouble.

Sunday 9th — Handed over Stores, Kit, etc to O.C. Details (Capt. Thomson).

3 pm. Capt. Sandeman & Lieut Gilkison joined

Sunday 9th (cont)   Capt. Muir, Lieuts. Bennett and W.G. Campbell left to assist training new Battalion at Depot.

Battalion paraded in 4 parties to leave FORT-GEORGE station at following hours.

1st Party. Lt.Col. Moulton-Barrett (I/c Train), Adjutant, Quartermaster, and Transport Officer, Sergt-Maj and 50 Headquarters.   6·10 pm.

2nd Party. Capt Hyslop (I/c Train) & B. Company 6·40 pm " Thorburn and A "

3rd Party. Major Maclean (I/c Train) & C Company Capt Fraser and D "

4th Party. Major Marshall (I/c Train) M.G. Officer and 50 Headquarters.

Transport Horses would not pull in the new harness and caused great delay, the difficulty of loading wagons also contributing to make the 1st Train 45 minutes late.

Monday 10th   1st Train arrived 12·30 pm, up to time, but succeeding trains were delayed outside SOUTHAMPTON DOCKS Station.

6·30 pm A and B Coys, on S.S. "SEAHOUND" steamed to BOULOGNE, the men being packed together.

1st Train Party and C. Company embarked S.S. "BERTHA", to sail at 10 pm, but hour of departure was postponed and men slept on board.

D Company and remainder of Headquarters

3

August.

Monday 10th (cont.) marched to a Rest Camp, about 3 miles out of SOUTHAMPTON, with 2nd Line Transport. A.S.C. Drivers reported.

Tuesday 11th 9 am. A and B Companies arrived BOULOGNE and marched to billets in the Old Barracks. Turned on at once to pitch tents for Rest Camps outside town.

5 pm. Headquarters and C Company arrived and joined A and B Companies.

Headquarters No 3 Base quartered in Hotel Bristol

Wednesday 12th Companies on Fatigue in Camps and at Docks.

Thursday 13th. Companies on Fatigue.
B Company moved to new Billets in the Girls School (ECOLE BRECQUERECQUE)

Friday 14th. Companies on Fatigue.
3 pm. D Company and remainder of Headquarters arrived on S.S. "Empress of India", and marched to billets in a school in PLACE FEMELONT)

Saturday 15th 9.30 pm. 3 Platoons, A Company (Capt Thorburn) were moved, with very little warning, to Railhead to assist loading etc. Lieuts Burt, Marshall, Ayton, and 2/Lieut Anderson, were in command of the Platoons
Companies on Fatigue.

Sunday 16th 10 am English Church Parade (Rev. Mr. Cassidy)

Monday 17th 10 am Battalion Parade, Section rushes and fire discipline. Companies on Fatigue.

4

August.

Tuesday 18th 6 am. Route March, returning at 9:15 am.
Companies on Fatigue.
7 pm. Concert given in Gymnasium by Residents, under the guidance of Dr Phillips. An artiste from the Paris and Brussells Opera Houses sang with great beauty.

Wednesday 19th Companies on Fatigue
10 pm. All Officers and C Company attended the Bearing of the body of the late General J. Grierson from the train to a ship. A French Guard of Honour also paraded and gave the salute. A bearer party of 8 N.C.Os. 93rd Hrs. carried the coffin on board, the Pipers playing "The Flowers of the Forest."

Thursday 20th Companies on Fatigue
Orders received to move Battalion to Railhead on the 21st, but cancelled later.

Friday 21st Companies on Fatigue.
Ordered move up rail on the 22nd, to entrain at 8.30 pm.

Saturday 22nd Prepared for move.
3:30 pm Transport loaded.
5:45 pm Battalion marched to Station and entrained.
7.35 pm Train left for VALENCIENNES.

Sunday 23rd 7.12 am Arrived VALENCIENNES. Detrained and marched to School, where Capt Thorburn's 3 Platoons were already bivouacked. Rations were

August.
Sunday 23rd. issued and breakfasts cooked
The 19th Bde of Infantry completed formation.
  Brig Genl Drummond, Commdg.
  Major Johnstone   Brig. Maj.
  Capt Jack, Cameronians. Staff Capt.
  Capt Turner.   A.D.C.
  Lieut Churchill.   Bde Sig Offr
1/ Middlesex. Lt. Col. Ward.
2/ Royal Welsh Fusiliers. Lt. Col. Delmé Radcliffe.
1/ Scottish Rifles, Cameronians. Lt. Col. Robertson.
2/ Arg. & Suthd. Highrs. Lt. Col. Moulton-Barrett.
19th Bde. Ammunition Column.

11am. Ordered march to ONNAING, where Bn. arrived 1pm. Artillery Fire heard from the direction of MONS.

2pm. Marched on to QUIÉVRECHAIN, C Company acting as advanced Guard, where Bn went into billets in an Iron Foundry. 6pm. C. Company halted, in Belgian territory, in QUIÉVRAIN.

6pm. C. Company found 2 picquets, Lieut A.K. MacLean and No.12 Platoon on frontier in QUIÉVRAIN, and 2/Lieut C.L. Campbell and No.11 Platoon at the Railway Crossing N of QUIÉVRECHAIN.

  The 1/ Middlesex and Cameronians were in position watching the Canal, with the R.W.Fus. in support in QUAROUBLE

8pm. D. Company ordered out to HENSIES to

6

August.
Sunday 23rd (cont) support the first line.
    12 mn. Middlesex reported "hard pressed".
    Brigade ordered to parade 2 am 24th to march
    to ELOUGES via QUIÉVRAIN.

Monday 24th 1 am. 2nd Line Transport and Ammunition
    Column moved off.
    2 am. Battalion moved off but halted
    at cross-roads in QUIÉVRECHAIN to allow rest
    of Brigade to pass through. Lieut. Maclean's
    Picquet ordered rejoin. Lieut. Campbell's Picquet
    ordered move to ST. HOMME to cover march of
    Brigade along road S. of Railway.
    4.30 am. Rest of Brigade through, but
    moved S from QUIÉVRAIN. Bn. marched on
    with B. Company as Rear-guard.
    8 am. Brigade halted in BAISIEUX.
    9 am. Brigade turned about and moved
    W. on ROMBIES.
    11 am. Brigade halted and took up a
    position facing N, 93rd Btn on the left of
    the line (vide sketch)

August
Monday 24ᵗʰ (cont.)   A, B, C, & D Companies, with the Machine Gun on the extreme left flank, were in first line, in trenches dug with the entrenching implement, while B Company remained in Reserve.

Our Cavalry and Artillery were in action in front of position but the Brigade was not attacked.

2 pm. Brigade moved on to JENLAIN, Battalion arriving at 4 pm. and prepared to bivouac in a field just N of the village, in the section of a position to be held by it.

5 pm. Orders re position cancelled. Battn ordered to move at once to occupy trenches prepared by the French on the high ground S.W. of ETH. 4ᵗʰ Hussars holding the line till Battn arrived, then moved back to occupy second line to the right. A and D Companies occupied the first line with B and C Companies in support. Communication established with the Cameronians on the left. Orders received that this position must be held at all costs. No supplies received so men without food.

10 pm. 2nd Line Transport arrived having been misdirected and made to cover 40 miles, moving at one point between the

August.

Monday 24ᵗʰ (cont) firing lines. Horses done up, and only Biscuits and tea on wagons.
2/Lieut Campbell and No 11 Platoon, less 15 N.C.Os and men, joined. When holding railway line at ST HOMME in conjunction with Cavalry was heavily attacked by a greatly superior force of German Infantry, and after a sharp fight was forced to fall back towards ELOUGES. Ptes. Rodger and Cassidy were killed, and 13 others wounded.

Tuesday 25ᵗʰ 1 am. Biscuits and hot tea issued.
4 am. Battalion formed up and joined Brigade in JENLAIN on march to HAUSSY. 2nd Line Transport moved very slowly as the horses were very done, and when German Cavalry came up Officers' Kits and the Adjutant's box were thrown off to lighten the load. Horses wouldn't pull so traces were cut and wagon set alight.
12·30 pm. Arrived HAUSSY, observed by German Aeroplane, and halted on slope of ridge N.W. of village. Arranged with inhabitants to supply hot meal for men, but hostile cavalry and guns forced our Cavalry back and the Brigade fell in and lined the ridge to oppose any attack
2 pm. Brigade withdrew and marched off to SOLESMES, covered by A Company as

August

Tuesday 25th (cont) rearguard. Two men were badly wounded by shrapnel (Ptes Docherty and Miller) when falling back

3.30 pm. Marched on from SOLESMES to LE CATEAU, arriving at 8 pm after very trying march in rain.

10 pm. Moved into billets, 1½ miles from Town square, in a factory near the Railway Station. Men very crowded and without food. A Company remained in billets in LE CATEAU with the Transport.

Wednesday 26th 4 am. Brigade stood to arms. A small ration of Bully Beef and Tea was issued and a meagre breakfast cooked.

5.10 am. Battalion marched into LE CATEAU and took place at the head of the Brigade. "A" Company joined in Square having been ordered to fall in with bayonets fixed as Uhlans were reported to have gained access to the Town. Capt. Thorburn went sick with fever.

5.30 am. Marched off to ESTRÉES

6.15 am. Ordered open out to Artillery formation and march on, Transport holding to the road

7 am. Closed on road and moved to Wood 400ˣ W of road. Brigade formed up.

10

August
Wednesday 26th (cont) 9 am. Heavy artillery fire was heard to the north. The Brigade was ordered to move E across the LE CATEAU — ESTREES road in support of the 5th Division. 2 Companies of the Royal Scots Fusiliers, which had lost touch with the headquarters of their Battalion and were temporarily attached to the 19th Bde, led the way. The "93rd" followed the first line, with the Royal Welsh Fusiliers in support; the Battalion moving in artillery formation, in order "C", "D", "B", and "A" Companies. After crossing the road the Battn was halted and the men lay down. A heavy Artillery duel was now in progress. Genl. Drummond issued the news that 40,000 French troops were moving from ARRAS on CAMBRAI against the German right flank.

11. am   Orders received "The Battn is to adv. at once in support of the Suffolk and Manchester Regts."

+ . The direction of the advance was now N.E. and "C" Company were ordered to halt on the S. slope of the ridge overlooking LE CATEAU, on the forward slope of which the firing line was lying under shell fire. "D" Company was moved up on the right of "C" Company with "A"

11

August

Wednesday, 26th (cont) Company (Less 1 Platoon, under Lieut. Burt Marshall, on Baggage Guard with the 2nd Line Train) in support, B Company supporting "C" Company. The men put up cover with their entrenching implements, but as yet they had not come under direct fire, though unaimed fire threatened to cause casualties.

Major MacLean (O.C. "C" Coy), could find no continuation of the firing line to the right front so ordered Lieut. A.K. MacLean to move with a patrol over the ridge and observe the ground on the forward slope.

12 noon. The firing line retired on the Battn. The ridge was covered by shell fire and a Field Battery on the left was forced to abandon its guns. "C" Coy moved forward to the ridge and came under a fierce artillery fire, while B Coy. in support suffered also as much from reverse and enfilade fire as from frontal fire. A Coy was deflected to the extreme left flank and moved rapidly forward, over the ridge, only to come under a heavy rifle and machine gun fire at short range.

1 pm. A Coy, having lost Capt. Walker, Lieut. Ayloun, and many men, was

12

August.

Wednesday 26th (cont) ordered back (in error) behind "D" Coy to reform. The Field Battery made a brave attempt to recover their guns, the teams galopping from well back right up to the ridge under fire, two of them succeeding in hooking in and getting away.

Col. Moulton Barrett ordered "A" Coy forward again, and led by Lieut. Aytoun the men went back into the fire and engaged the opposing Infantry

1.30 pm. Maj. Maclean led an advance of 2 Platoons of "C" Coy (Capt. Bruce, Lieuts Gilbison) and 2 Platoons of "B" Coy (Capts. Maclean & Kennedy, and Lieut Connal Rowan) to the N, right through the shell fire against the German Infantry, while Capt. Hyslop (O.C. "B" Coy) brought forward the remaining Platoons of B and C. Coys. to the forward slope of the ridge. The Manchesters and Suffolks fell right back, and a re-inforcing movement by the 1/Middlesex did not bring any result. The Machine Gun, which had come into action on the right at very long range, could not get effect and could not be advanced to a more forward position, as the enemy's shell fire dominated the ground and opened quickly and accurately on every visible target.

Capt Henderson with men of "A" and "D" Coys moved down on the right into the valley towards the Railway line and

August   13

Wednesday 26th (cont) in conjunction with a small party of the Middlesex prepared to push on up the far slope. Capt. Hyslop covered this advance with fire, but the O.C. Middlesex ordered Capt. Henderson to fall back to the ridge, and the party suffered some loss in doing so.

3 pm. Capt. Hyslop's party, lying amongst corn stooks on the forward slope, was suffering little loss and by its fire held up the German Infantry in an Iron Foundry range 900 yds. Various attempted forward movements at longer ranges were also stopped.

5 pm. Communication with Maj. Maclean had been lost, and all troops to the W. had retired from view, so Capt. Hyslop, seeing that his position was isolated, decided to fall back S. to the next ridge where he formed a force consisting of his own men, a party of R.E., and stragglers from other units, to hold this position. On the way Lieut. Stirling (Machine Gun Officer) was picked up, wounded in 4 places, and carried back to the temporary hospital in REUMONT Church.

Meanwhile Col. Moulton Barrett had collected a small force consisting

14

August.
Wednesday 26th (cont.) of 2 Platoons of D Coy, men of A Coy, and men of the Scots Fusiliers and Middlesex Regt., and took up a position on a ridge to the E of REUMONT, in line with the Norfolk Regt on the right. It was clear that all British troops in this area of the battle had fallen back, and as a German force was observed moving S. along the railway Col. Moulton-Barrett despatched in turn Maj. Marshall and Capt. Henderson to ascertain what orders had been issued to the Brigade. The Staff Captain, 19th Brigade, alone was on the field.

6 p.m. A counter-attack ordered by the G.O.C. 5th Division could not be carried out, so Col. Moulton-Barrett, seeing that he must give way in face of the German flanking movement, which was in very strong force, fell back gradually to the high ground N.W. of HONNECHY and then moved S to the railway line and followed the line till within 1 mile of as far as BUSIGNY. The Royal Welsh Fusiliers had taken up a position about 1 mile N of BUSIGNY to cover the retirement.

Capt. Hyslop, also anticipating the German movement on the E, and

August.

Wednesday 26th (cont.) acting under instructions received from the O.C. Middlesex, fell back through REUMONT to the W of the village and then regained the main road, marching on towards ESTRÉES

10 pm Capt. Hyslop collected all men of the Battalion as they came into ESTRÉES and they lay down in the Square and slept. The road was blocked with Transport and a continuous stream of men of various units poured into the village

10.30 pm Col. Moulton Barrett's party arrived BEAUREVOIR, having been directed there to find the rest of the Battalion. Halted and men slept.

11 pm. Capt. Hyslop, with Capt. Henderson, (who had missed Col. Moulton Barrett's party in the darkness) Lieuts. Clark, Johnstone, Rose, St. Clair, 2/Lieuts. C. L. Campbell, Stewart, H. A. Campbell, Hetherington-haugh, Lieut Buffner R.A.M.C. and Buchanan, and about 200 men marched on to ST. QUENTIN. Lieut Aitken, 2/Lieut Anderson and about 150 men had been led to a field E of ESTRÉES by a Staff Officer and informed that the Battn would form up there. As the Transport was completely blocked, Capt Hyslop was ordered to take out the teams and lead

August.

Wednesday 26th (Cont) them, abandoning 1 Water Cart, 5 S.A.A. Carts, and 1 G.S. Limbered Wagon.

The Battalion was now split up into 3 parties and though every effort was made by the Officers i/c these parties to join Battn. Headquarters they were kept apart till the 5th Sept. The party which Major Maclean led to the attack about 1.30 p.m. was not seen again and all the officers there are missing. This party, though checked by the heavy shell fire from the German Artillery to the N and W, and when called on to go forward again went straight through the storm of fire past the retreating firing line, and forced an attack against the German infantry advancing from LE CATEAU. A Coy. went back a second time into the hail of fire when ordered and held up the vastly superior forces opposed to them.

Thursday 27th 12.15 am. Major Lt. Col. Moulton-Barrett's party marched from BEAUREVOIR, with the 5th Division, via HARGICOURT (where Major Marshall took over command, Col. Moulton-Barrett going to NOYON) to VERMAND. 11 pm. Marched towards HAM.

August.

Thursday 27th (cont) Capt. Hyslop's Party.

3 am. Arrived outside ST QUENTIN and ordered to halt and lie down by the road side. Men very done, and slept where they lay.

5 am. Ordered march into town. Halted at Railway Stn, where Staff asked whether party could move right on to NOYON by road. Impossible march on without food and rest as men had eaten nothing since 4 am, 26th. Party marched to field near Station and given a good meal of Tea and Bread.

9 am. Ordered entrain for NOYON. Joined by party of 50 men, Cook's wagon, 1 S.A.A. Cart, 1 Water Cart, 1 Limbered Wagon, and Machine Gun and Wagon.

10 am. Train left for NOYON. Had to leave S.A.A. Cart, Water Cart, and Limbered Wagon behind as no room on train, but brought on all horses. Men drew full Rations. Genl. Drummond on train.

11.30 am. Arrived NOYON. Officers and 150 men detrained, but owing to Staff Error the remainder of the Party were not allowed to get out, nor could the vehicles be moved.

18

August.
Thursday 27th (cont). 12 noon. Marched up to Cavalry Barracks with large party of Details and bedded down in 2 Riding Schools.

Lieut. Burt-Marshall and his Platoon (Baggage Guard) with 2nd Line Transport arrived after a trying trek.

Lt-Col. Moulton-Barrett took command of the Party and formed Battn. Headquarters.

Lieut. Aitken's Party
1 am Left ESTRÉES by march route
8 am. Arrived ~~SOMPHE~~ ST. QUENTIN, and tried to find Capt Hyslop, but misdirected. Enemy's Artillery shelled ground close to Town.
11 am Marched on to ~~NOYON~~ HAM.
5 pm Arrived ~~NOYON~~ HAM, and halted by roadside, with 4th Division. Bivouacked in Field for night.

Capt. Henderson's Party.
12:30 pm. Capt Henderson was ordered by Col. Moulton-Barrett to take command of the party left on the train at NOYON. Left NOYON with 2/Lieut St. Clair and 2/Lieut. Stewart and men, now totalling about 150 all ranks.
1 pm. Arrived RIBÉCOURT, where informed the Battn would assemble to rest and refit.

19

August.
Friday 28th. Ordered parade 9.30 am march to PONTOISE
Supplies issued en route. Lt. Rose went sick.
10.30 am Arrived PONTOISE. 17th Bde
Headquarters formed, and Brigade assembled
in village. Battn billeted, and found a
Picquet, 6 N.C.Os and 24 men, to guard Swing
Bridge over R. OISE.

          Major Marshall's Party.
8.30 am Arrived HAM. Bread procured and
men breakfasted.
11 am. Marched on, attached to Gordon
Highlanders. Brig. Genl Doran sent 20
men, unfit to march, by motor-lorry.

          Capt. Henderson's Party.
Rested at RIBÉCOURT. Could get no orders
as to how or where I must join the
Battn.

          Lieut. Aitken's Party.
4.30 am Division started for NOYON.
9.30 am Party, as Rear-guard to Division
left ~~NOYON~~ @ HAM.
3 pm. Arrived NOYON and halted by
roadside. Could get no information as
to whereabouts of Battalion.
6 pm. Entrained and left for COMPIÉGNE
7 pm. Arrived COMPIÉGNE. Party slept
in Hangars.

August
Saturday 29th. Men rested and cleaned up kit.
7 pm. Battn paraded with Bde.
8.30 pm Marched off to LAIGLE.
12 mn Arrived LAIGLE. 50 men billeted in shed, remainder slept on road

    Major Marshall's Party.
Marched to GENVRY.

    Capt. Henderson's Party
& Section A, 19th Field Amb. attached to party.
Party entrained for COMPIÈGNE.
Arrived COMPIÈGNE, but engine driver started off again before the men could detrain and only stopped at BEAUVAIS. Capt. Henderson demanded return to COMPIÈGNE and train ran back.

    Lieut Aitken's Party.
Rested at COMPIÈGNE, moving out to Rest Camp. Lieut. Rose joined and took over command.

August.
Sunday 30th 5 am. Ordered move COULOISY, via CARLEPONT and ATTICHY.

    5.45 am. Marched at head of Brigade.
    8 am. Halted, after very slow march, 2 miles E by S of CARLEPONT. Rations issued and breakfasts cooked.
    9.30 am. Continued march.
    5.30 pm. Arrived COULOISY. Officers billeted in Mairie. Men bivouacked on field.

        Major Marshall's Party
2 pm. Marched to COURTIEUX.

        Capt. Henderson's Party.
On reporting to Lt. Col. Cavendish, A.A.G. G.H.Q. received orders to go by train to CRÉPY-en-VALOIS.

        Lieut. Rose's Party.
4 am. Left COMPIÈGNE by train.
4 pm. Arrived ROUEN
11 pm. Left ROUEN by train.

August
Monday. 31st   5 a.m. Paraded at head of Brigade.
Lieut & Qrmr Clayton, kicked on leg by a horse,
and 2/Lieut. H.A. Campbell sent to Base, sick.
6 a.m. Marched off en route for VERBERIE.
12 noon. Sent out as Right Flank Guard as
Uhlans reported to have crossed R. AISNE.
On reaching the PARIS route turned S as
Rear Guard, but the 12th Brigade cut in in
front of us.
8 p.m. Arrived VERBERIE, to find that
billets were near SALINES, about 1½ miles
out of town. Retraced steps and followed
up road in dark.
10.30 p.m. Arrived SALINES, men very tired,
so got them into billets.
   Major Marshall's Party.
3.45 a.m. Left COURTIEUX. Maj. Marshall
rode to COULOISY and found Battn. Headqrs.
Arranged join Battn at ETIENNE.
 Staff Officer ordered Party not to march
to join 19th Bde as hostile Cavalry reported
to be between the Columns. Marched to CREPY.
   Capt. Henderson's Party.
A.G. at ~~COMPIEGNE~~ CREPY-en-VALOIS informed
that the 2nd Army Corps would pass through
and that Capt. Henderson must join it,
though 19th Brigade now belonged to the 3rd
Army Corps.   Marched men to a place

August

Monday 31st (cont.) where the men could wash and cook. 2nd Army Corps arrived in evening, so party moved to camp close to it and reported. Major Marshall reported to be with Corps.

Lieut Rose's party.
8.30 pm. Arrived LE MANS. Marched to Rest Camp at CASERNE CHANZY.

SEPTMONTS
2nd Oct. 1914.

[signature] Lt. Col.
Commdg. 2/Arg & Suthd. Highrs

19th Infantry Brigade.

2nd BATTALION

ARGYLL & SUTHERLAND HIGHLANDERS

SEPTEMBER 1914

INTELLIGENCE SUMMARY.

(Erase heading not required.)

Instructions regarding War Diaries and Intelligence Summaries are contained in F.S. Regs., Part II. and the Staff Manual respectively. Title pages will be prepared in manuscript.

Hour, Date, Place			Summary of Events and Information	Remarks and references to Appendices
3 am	1st September	SALINES	Supply column moving S. through village. 3 Uhlans rode in from the N. and fired down the street, hitting Pte FEATHERSTONHAUGH's horse. Battalion fell in an alarm posts, but Uhlans had cleared off.	
4 am	"	"	No return, but CAMERONIANS stood to.	
4.30 am	"	"	Artillery fire heard from S.E. Ordered one Coy to ridge S.E. to help Cavalry, also took up position on left of 13 Brigade (19th). Thick mist encountered. Difficulty of situation as little information was to hand.	
5.30 am	"	"	1/MIDDLESEX and CAMERONIANS pushed on towards NERY.	
6 am	"	"	Ordered to follow up towards NERY.	
7 am	"	NERY.	Halted in NERY. Village a shambles. QUEEN'S BAYS and L. BATTERY R.H.A. shelled in billets and suffered heavily till relieved by 1/MIDDLESEX advance which captured German guns and about 30 prisoners.	
8 am	"	"	19th Left Bde. passed Coy Bde. and fell back on FRESNOY expecting attack, but Germans did not follow up.	
1 pm	"	FRESNOY.	Formed up on ridge S. of village and rested.	
3-1/2 pm	"	"	Bde. ordered to take up Outpost position on ridge, covering BARON. 7th Coy sent Wr to cover left flank so dug in with entrenching implements and awaited attack.	
5 am	2nd "	FRESNOY	Withdrew from position and marched to BARON.	ⓂⒶ
7 am	"	BARON	Halted and cooked breakfasts. Bde. formed up.	
8 am	"	"	Marched at head of Bde. to EVE.	
11 am	"	EVE	Halted N. of village, where Artillery blocked street	ⓂⒶ

Forms/C. 2118/10.

INTELLIGENCE SUMMARY.

(Erase heading not required.)

Instructions regarding War Diaries and Intelligence Summaries are contained in F.S. Regs., Part II. and the Staff Manual respectively. Title pages will be prepared in manuscript.

Hour, Date, Place		Summary of Events and Information	Remarks and references to Appendices
1.30 pm	2nd September, ÈVE	Germans reported advancing, so orders issued Bde take up a defensive position to cover village, Loppin. Sehtd Bde in support.	
2 pm	"	No attack, orders cancelled.	
3 pm	"	Marched on via DAMMARTIN to LONGPERRIER.	
6 pm	" LONGPERRIER	Moved out 1½ mile N.W. to take up section of Outpost Line, 1 Plan C Coy (2nd Lt Campbell c.) in position.	(Sgd) H.
12.30 am	3rd "	Marched to DAMMARTIN, where 19th Bde joined 4th Division in march on LAGNY.	
10 am	LAGNY	Halted and cooked breakfasts.	
1 pm	"	Marched out to Bivouac 1½ miles E of town.	(Sgd) H.
2 am	4th "	Rested in Bivouac.	(Sgd) H.
5 am	"	Marched in rear of Bde via LA FERRIÈRE to GRISSY.	
9.30 am	GRISSY	Halted in Farm where breakfasts were cooked. Party of 200 men under Major MARSHALL, Capt. HENDERSON, Lt. St. CLAIR, 2/Lieut. STEWART, joined Headquarters from JOSSIGNY.	
11 am	"	Moved to Bivouac in Orchard at W end of village.	
1.7 pm	"	Party of 184 men under Lieuts ROSE & AITKEN, 2/Lieut ANDERSON joined Headquarters from LE MANS	
4 pm	"	Taquet in Outpost Line. (30 N.C.Os & men under 2/Lieut ANDERSON)	
6 pm	"	Capt. M.G. SANDEMAN reported arrival of 1st Reinforcement (1 Officer & 94 N.C.Os & men) in CHERY.	(Sgd) H.
7 pm	"		

INTELLIGENCE SUMMARY.

(Erase heading not required.)

Instructions regarding War Diaries and Intelligence Summaries are contained in F.S. Regs., Part II. and the Staff Manual respectively. Title pages will be prepared in manuscript.

Hour, Date, Place	Summary of Events and Information	Remarks and references to Appendices
6.30 am. 6th September 1914 ANNEX	Headquarters with "A" & "B" Companies marched to OZOIR-LA-FERRIÉRE via	
10 am " OZOIR-LA-FERRIÉRE	guard Bde. Supply Column. Bivouacked first W of outskirts village	
7.30 am "	"C" & "D" Companies under Major K. MARSHALL marched to BRIE COMTE ROBERT to guard Bde. Ammn. Column.	
8.30 am 7th October "	Headquarters with "A" and "B" Companies marched to catch up 19th Bde., already advancing N.E. with the 3rd Corps. Route via VILLENEUVE ST DENIS — MONTBARBIN — SANCY — LA HAUTE MAISON	
8 pm " LA HAUTE MAISON	Bivouacked with Bde. Lieut J.A. LIDDELL with 3rd Reinforcement (84 N.C.Os & men) reported arrival.	
11 pm " "	Major MARSHALL with C & D Companies marched in	
4 am 8th "	Paraded in reserve to Bde. which moved very slowly N.E. towards LA FERTÉ	
10 am SIGNY	Battn. moved up to act with ROYAL WELSH FUSILIERS in attack on infade enemy occupying S of F. MARNE. High ground S of LA FERTÉ occupied without resistance.	
5 pm " CH. VENTEUIL	B & C Companies moved forward to take up position covering S. bank of R.MARNE in LA FERTÉ and came under mobile rifle and Machine gun fire from N. bank. Pte. Butterworth (B.Coy) wounded.	
7 pm " "	B Coy. found Outposts on line of defence. ROYAL WELSH FUSILIERS	
11 pm " "	pushed forward into LA FERTÉ. "C" Coy relieved "B" Coy.	

Form C. 2118/10.

INTELLIGENCE SUMMARY.

(Erase heading not required.)

Instructions regarding War Diaries and Intelligence Summaries are contained in F.S. Regs., Part II. and the Staff Manual respectively. Title pages will be prepared in manuscript.

Hour, Date, Place			Summary of Events and Information	Remarks and references to Appendices
5.30 am	9th September	CH. VENTEUIL	"C" Coy. fell back, under heavy fire, on Battn. Ordered wait till ROYAL WELSH FUSILIERS arrived. ROYAL WELSH FUSILIERS relieved in LA FERTÉ and join them to return to 19th Bde. at SIGNY.	
10 am	"	"	ROYAL WELSH FUSILIERS arrived. Marched together to SIGNY.	
12.30 pm	"	SIGNY.	Halted, cooked dinners, and awaited orders.	
7 pm	"	"	Marched at head of Bde. to JOUARRE.	
8.30 pm	"	JOUARRE.	Halted. Men lay down to rest.	
12.30 am	10th	"	Marched through LA FERTÉ, crossed R MARNE by Pontoon Bridge to MARCY Fm	[Appx] 4
9 am	"	MARCY Fm	Marched on to CERTIGNY	
11 am	"	"		
4.30 pm	"	CERTIGNY	Halted and bivouacked on field for the night.	[Appx] 4
6.30 am	11th	"	Marched for destination LA CROCHE Fm	
1 pm	"	PASSY EN VALOIS	Halted just S of town to allow 12th Bde. to pass on front. Heavy Rain storm caused men to strew. Moved on through PASSY	
2 pm	"	"	Halted, men went into billets for night. Clear weather	[Appx] 4
8.30 pm	"	MARITZY ST GENEVIÈVE		
5.30 am	12th	"	Marched at head of Bde. "C" Coy formed Adv. Gd. Roads very heavy as result of rain. Heavy firing towards CHAUDUN where 4 Divn in contact with enemy.	
3 pm	"	BUZANCY	Halted and billeted. Rain falling heavily	[Appx] 4
10 am	13th	"		[Appx] 4
12 noon	"	"	As operations reported moving slowly 13th ordered rest till afternoon. Orders received 12.30 pm to continue advance.	

INTELLIGENCE SUMMARY.

Instructions regarding War Diaries and Intelligence Summaries are contained in F.S. Regs., Part II. and the Staff Manual respectively. Title pages will be prepared in manuscript.

(Erase heading not required.)

Hour, Date, Place	Summary of Events and Information	Remarks and references to Appendices
12.30 pm – 3 pm 13th September BOZANCY SEPTMONTS	Marched in rear of Bde. Halted just N of village and bivouacked in field.	Offr. L.
12.15 am 14th " "	Marched to bivouack at crossroads 1 mile S of VENIZEL. Raining heavily.	
2 pm " " VENIZEL	Crossed 400 W of Bivouack shelled. No damage. MIDDLESEX and CAMERONIANS crossing to N bank of R. AISNE.	Offr. L.
2.30 am 15th " "	Marched through VENIZEL to a wood ½ mile N of Ribecon Bridge. Enemy's shells found overhead through the day.	
7 pm " " 10 pm " " 10.30 pm " "	B, C, D Coys dug deep trenches. A Coy in reserve. Raining heavily. Orders received move to BUCY-LE-LONG, present to 11th Bde. Move cancelled.	Offr. L. Offr. L.
6 pm " " 16th " " 8.30 pm " "	Ordered move BUCY-LE-LONG reserve to 10th Bde. Marched under cover of darkness to BUCY-LE-LONG and bivouacked in field just S of village, relieving WARWICKSHIRE Regt.	
10 am " " 17th " " BUCY-LE-LONG	Reform C Coy and Section each A, B, & D Coys sent out to clear up village, bring men & horses etc. Remainder improved bivouack.	
11 am " " " "	Enemy's siege guns suddenly opened on bivouack. Battalion moved from field as quickly as possible, leaving transport wagons and carts. 5 horses hit. 2nd Lieut. McQueen, B Coy shot in head, Pte McCafferty and Kinsella lightly wounded. Battn. formed up in orchard at E end of village. Shelling this severe. Transport carts etc recovered under cover at W end of LA MARGUERITE. Raining heavily.	Offr. L.
12 noon " " LA MARGUERITE		

INTELLIGENCE SUMMARY.

(Erase heading not required.)

Instructions regarding War Diaries and Intelligence Summaries are contained in F. S. Regs., Part II. and the Staff Manual respectively. Title pages will be prepared in manuscript.

Hour, Date, Place	Summary of Events and Information	Remarks and references to Appendices
3 pm 17th September. BUCY-LE-LONG	Battalion occupied Bivouacs E of village. Hostile shell fire continued at intervals throughout the day.	Ap H
10 am 18th " "	4 Fatigue Parties (1 Platoon per Coy) sent out to clean up and bury dead in village. Remainder of Battn rested in Bivouack.	Ap H
12.30 am 19th " "	Capts Ure, Moorhouse & Lothian Lidderdale, Lord Erskine, 3/A.& S. Hrs. and 2/Lieut. Blacklock, 1/A.& S. Hrs. joined from Base and were taken on the strength.	
" " "	Parties for cleaning up and more collecting worked during the day. Rain fell heavily.	Ap H
10 am 20th " "	"A" Coy. went out to refix road S. of village. Fatigue parties worked through the day. Heavy rain and bivouacks very damp.	Ap H
10 am 21st " "	Fatigue parties out to clean up and collect material for obstacles.	
7.30 pm " "	Marched to join 19th Bde at VENIZEL. Heavy rifle fire broke out in line held by 10th Bde.	
8.30 pm " VENIZEL	On reaching River Bridge ordered stand fast in case 4th Div in need of assistance	Ap H

INTELLIGENCE SUMMARY.

(Erase heading not required.)

Instructions regarding War Diaries and Intelligence Summaries are contained in F. S. Regs., Part II. and the Staff Manual respectively. Title pages will be prepared in manuscript.

Hour, Date, Place	Summary of Events and Information	Remarks and references to Appendices
10 pm 21st September VENIZEL	Marched on, in rear of Bde. to SEPTMONTS. Heavy showers fell [raining]	M.4
12.5 am 22nd SEPTMONTS	Halted. Men moved into billets. Lieut PURVES and 2nd Re-inforcement (100 N.C.Os & men), already in billets, reported for duty.	
7.30 am "	"A" and "B" Coys paraded with entrenching tools and proceeded to ACY to dig trenches.	
12.15 pm "	"C" Coy marched to relieve "B" Coy	
2 pm "	"D" Coy marched to relieve "A" Coy	
6 pm "	"C" & "D" Coys returned. New Machine Guns and Limbered Wagon received.	M.4
10 am 23rd "	Coy Parades	
2.30 pm "	Coy Parades	
11.30 pm "	Lieuts MACPHERSON & FAIRLIE and 2/Lieut CUNNINGHAM with 4th Reinforcement (128 N.C.Os & men) joined Battalion from the Base.	M.4
10 am 24th "	Coy Parades	
2.30 pm "	Coy Parades	M.4
10 am 26th "	"A", "B", & "C" Coy Parades	M.4
12.15 pm "	"D" Coy marched to dig trenches	M.4

INTELLIGENCE SUMMARY.
(Erase heading not required.)

Instructions regarding War Diaries and Intelligence Summaries are contained in F.S. Regs., Part II. and the Staff Manual respectively. Title pages will be prepared in manuscript.

Hour, Date, Place	Summary of Events and Information	Remarks and references to Appendices
2.30 pm 25th September SEPTMONTS	"A", "B", & "C" Coy Parade	
10 am 26th "	Coy Parade	A.H
2.30 pm " "	Coy Parades	A.H
5.45 am 27th "	Orders parade at once. Enemy reported crossing R. AISNE opposite the 5th Division	A.H
6.20 am " "	Parade dismissed, Battn. ready to move off. Brigade ordered to stand to arms at 5 am daily.	
11 am " "	Presbyterian Service, conducted by G.O.C. 19th Bde., in orchard at E. end of village	
5 am 28th "	Stood to arms till 6 am.	A.H
10 am " "	Battalion Route March	
2.30 pm " "	Coy Parades. "C" Coy marched to dig Trenches.	A.H
5 am 29th "	Stood to arms till 6 am.	
8 am " "	1 Platoon "A" Coy marched to dig gunpits for "Heavies".	
10 am " "	Coy Parades	
2.30 pm " "	Coy Parade	

INTELLIGENCE SUMMARY.

(Erase heading not required.)

Instructions regarding War Diaries and Intelligence Summaries are contained in F. S. Regs., Part II. and the Staff Manual respectively. Title pages will be prepared in manuscript.

Hour, Date, Place	Summary of Events and Information	Remarks and references to Appendices
5 am. 30th September SEPTMONTS	Stood to arms till 6 am.	
7.20am. "	"B" Coy paraded and marched to dig trenches.	
10 am. "	"A", "C", & "D" Coys Parade.	
2.30 pm. "	"A", "C", & "D" Coy. Parade.	

INTELLIGENCE SUMMARY.

(Erase heading not required.)

Hour, Date, Place		Summary of Events and Information	Remarks and references to Appendices
1st September	CRÉPY-EN-VALOIS	Major Marshall's Party. Joined Party under Capt. HENDERSON. Major Marshall took command	@ H
2nd "	NANTEUIL	Arrived by march route as a separate unit attached 2nd Army Corps.	@ H
		19th Field Ambulance joined forces	@ H
3rd "	MONTYON	Marched in and attached to Army Troops.	@ H
4th "	VILLIERS S/MORIN	Arrived by march route	@ H
7.30pm "		Marched to JOSSIGNY	@ H
3.30am 5th "	JOSSIGNY	Marched to GRISSY	@ H
11am @	GRISSY	Rejoined Battalion.	@ H
		Lieut Rose's Party	
1st September	LE MANS	Paraded with details for outfitting	@ H
2nd "	"	"	@ H
3rd "	"	"	@ H
9.30pm "	"	Paraded with details R.Warwickshire and WILTSHIRE Regts. Marched to station	@ H
4am 4th "	"	Train left. Journey via TOURS and ORLEANS.	@ H
4pm 5th "	GRISSY	Rejoined Battalion.	@ H

6th December, 1914.

[signature] Clark Lieut
9th Arg, Suthd. Hrs.

19th Infantry Brigade.

2nd BATTALION

ARGYLE & SUTHERLAND HIGHLANDERS

(OCTOBER 1914

121/36/3

== Confidential. ==

== War Diary ==

— of —

== 2nd Battalion Argyll & Sutherland Highlanders ==
== 19th Brigade ==

From 1st October 1914 to 31st October 1914

(Volume 3)

Index.

	Pages.
Summary of Events and Information,	1 to 20,
Appendix A1.	21 & 22,
Appendix A2.	23.
Appendix A3.	24,
Appendix A4.	25.
Appendix A5.	26,
Appendix B. (Sketch)	27,

Army Form C. 2118.

WAR DIARY
or
INTELLIGENCE SUMMARY.
(Erase heading not required.)

Instructions regarding War Diaries and Intelligence Summaries are contained in F.S. Regs., Part II. and the Staff Manual respectively. Title pages will be prepared in manuscript.

Hour, Date, Place	Summary of Events and Information	Remarks and references to Appendices
5am 1st October SEPTEMBER	Stood to arms till 6 am.	
10 am " "	Coy. Parade	
2.30 pm " "	Coy. Parade	
5 am 2nd "	Stood to arms till 6 am	
10 am " "	Coy. Parade	
2 pm " "	Coy. Parade	
5 am 3rd "	Stood to arms till 6 am	
10 am " "	Coy. Parades	
2 pm " "	Coy. Parades	
5 am 4th "	Stood to arms till 6 am	
6 am " "	"A" Coy marched to dig trenches 2 mile E. of VENIZEL. Shelled out and returned.	
10 am " "	Presbyterian Service conducted by O.C. 19th Bde.	
6 pm " "	"D" Coy marched to dig trenches	
11.55 pm " "	"D" Coy returned.	
5 am 5th "	Stood to arms till 6 am	

Forms/C. 2118/11
(B 29 6) W 2794 100,000 8/14 H W V

WAR DIARY
— OF —
INTELLIGENCE SUMMARY.
(Erase heading not required.)

Army Form C. 2118.

Instructions regarding War Diaries and Intelligence Summaries are contained in F.S. Regs., Part II. and the Staff Manual respectively. Title pages will be prepared in manuscript.

Hour, Date, Place	Summary of Events and Information	Remarks and references to Appendices
10 am. 5th October, SEPTMONTS.	Coy. Parades	
7.30 pm. " "	[Paraded with Bde.] Marched [in rear of Bde.] to ST REMY	(A)
2.30 am. 6th " ST REMY.	Halted. Bivouacked in a wood and kept under cover during the day.	(B)
7.30 pm. " "	Marched [at head of Bde.] for VEZ.	
2 am. 7th " — VEZ	Halted. Bivouacked under cover of trees	(C) q 3
5.30 pm. " "	[Paraded and] marched to BETHISY-ST-PIERRE.	
10 pm. " BETHISY-ST-PIERRE	Halted. Bivouacked under cover of trees. [Freezing hard and bitting cold.]	(D)
12.30 am. 8th " "	Marched [in head of Bde.] for entraining station, PONT-ST-MAXENCE.	
5 pm. " PONT-ST-MAXENCE	Bivouacked on ground S.W. of Station and prepared to entrain about 12 am.	(E)
8 pm. " "	Entraining orders cancelled	
7.50 am. 9th " "	Paraded, marched for next entraining station, ESTRÉES-ST-DENIS.	
12 noon. " ESTRÉES-ST-DENIS	Halted. Bivouacked on field S.W. of Station	
6.15 pm. " "	Transport moved to station and was entrained by "C" Coy.	
10 pm. " "	Bn. Hqrs, B, C Coy & 2 Platoons "D" Coy entrained in Bde 2nd Train	
10.40 pm. " "	Bde 2nd Train left. Route via AMIENS - ETAPLES.	

Army Form C. 2118.

WAR DIARY
—OF—
INTELLIGENCE SUMMARY.
(Erase heading not required.)

Instructions regarding War Diaries and Intelligence Summaries are contained in F.S. Regs., Part II. and the Staff Manual respectively. Title pages will be prepared in manuscript.

Hour, Date, Place		Summary of Events and Information	Remarks and references to Appendices
2 am	10th October, 1914 ESTRÉES-ST DENIS	Major Marshall, "A" Coy and 2 Platoons D Coy entrained in Bde. 3rd Train	(M)
2.45 am	"	Bde. 3rd Train left. (Route via ETAPLES – BOULOGNE – CALAIS)	
1.7 am	" BLENDEQUES	Bde. 2nd Train party detrained [carried by a party from the LONDON SCOTTISH]	
2.7 am	" "	Marched off to ST OMER	
3.15 pm	" ST OMER	Arrived and moved into billets in the Cavalry Barracks	
5 pm	" WATTEN	Bde. 3rd Train party detrained [Arrangements made to billet the Party but	9 3
		orders changed and Party ordered to march on ST OMER]	
11.55 pm	" ST OMER	3rd Train Party arrived and rejoined 2nd Train Party in billets	
5 am	11th "	Slept to arms till 5.15 am	(M)
7.30 am	" "	Marched at head of Brigade (B Coy as advanced guard)	
10 "	" FORT ROUGE	Halted in field and cooked dinner	
12.40 pm	" "	Marched on to RENESCURE (Pte BLACKLOCK)	
1.15 pm	" RENESCURE	Relieved the CAMERONIANS. "B" Coy found 1 Platoon on the HAZEBROUCK road	
		at the barricade & ends E of the village. Remainder of Battalion billeted in	
		village.	
5.30 am	12th "	Paraded to march in Brigade, which formed the Advanced Guard to the 6th	(M)

Army Form C. 2118.

WAR DIARY
of
INTELLIGENCE SUMMARY.
(Erase heading not required.)

Hour, Date, Place	Summary of Events and Information	Remarks and references to Appendices
5.30 am 12th October RENESCURE	Division - Route via EBBLINGHEM-HAZEBROUCK on STRAZEELE. Very cold, misty morning. French Territorials at work along roads digging trenches.	
8 am " " LES CINQ RUES	Ordered turn NE to HAZEBROUCK.	
9.30 am " " LA MOTTE	Halted. The mist lifted and "B" Coy put out posts on the roads leading E, SE, and W from the village. Battalion rested in a field N of the village. A British Cav. Bde was reported to be at SYLVESTRE and CAESTRE and German Cav. in the neighbourhood. Communication established with 1/ROYAL WELSH FUSILIERS in LA BRÉARDE, 1/MIDDLESEX in BORRE, and Bde Hdqrs. with the CAMERONIANS, at pt 26 on crossing N of BORRE.	
2.7 pm " " "	Ordered march on to EECKE and take up an outpost position to N and NE. "C" Company (Capt. SANDEMAN) detached to OOST LYNDHE.	
4.7 pm " " EECKE	Found 6 Battalion French Territorial Infantry halted in village and also the Light Cav. Divr. Field Ambulance. The G.O.C. French Infantry gave information that his troops were moving further N.W. Battalion took up an outpost position: Hdqrs. D Coy - A Coy - D Coy holding the line,	

WAR DIARY
or
INTELLIGENCE SUMMARY.
(Erase heading not required.)

Army Form C. 2118.

Hour, Date, Place	Summary of Events and Information	Remarks and references to Appendices
4 pm. 12th October. EECKE	and digging in. "B" Coy (less 1 Platoon) in Reserve in billets. French troops remained and bivouacked all round the village.	(M)
9.7 pm. "	Capt HERVEY, with a cyclist platoon, reported for temporary duty. A very cold night.	(M)
7.30 am 13th "	Marched off via CAESTRE, where "C" Coy rejoined, to ROUGE CROIX	
9.30 am ROUGE CROIX	Halted in field, where ROYAL WELSH FUSILIERS joined.	
9 am "	Moved on about 200x g. to a field where 19th Bde assembled	
9.30 am "	Marched on to field still further S (200x) on W side of CAESTRE-STRAZEELE road. Bde to form reserve to 6th Division in an attack against German line LES TROIS FERMES — LES 4 FILS D'AYMON	
1.30 pm "	Attack by 3rd Corps ordered. Raining heavily and artillery handicapped	
5 pm "	Battalion went into billets. Very wet and windy. Attack reported successful.	
5.20 am 14th "	Ordered to be ready to move at 10 minutes notice. 3rd Corps to resume attack	
11.30 am "	Marched in support to ROYAL WELSH FUSILIERS in attack on BAILLEUL	
12 noon "	Enemy reported to have retired from BAILLEUL. March to be continued on NIEPPE, the 18th Bde on the right moving on STEENWERK, the 4th Div.	

Army Form C. 2118.

WAR DIARY
or
INTELLIGENCE SUMMARY.
(Erase heading not required.)

Instructions regarding War Diaries and Intelligence Summaries are contained in F. S. Regs., Part II. and the Staff Manual respectively. Title pages will be prepared in manuscript.

Hour, Date, Place	Summary of Events and Information	Remarks and references to Appendices
12 noon 14th October	Operating on the left. 1/ROYAL WELSH FUSILIERS, on advanced guard, came in contact with double patrols near LE LEUTHE Fme	(10)
3.7pm LE LEUTHE Fme	Halted. "B" Coy sent out 1 Platoon (2/Lieut CUNNINGHAM) to watch right flank.	
7pm "	Marched to bivouac W. of MONT NILE. 1 Platoon "C" Coy (2/Lt Campbell) took post on road to BAILLEUL STN.	
9pm MONT NILE	Bivouacked for the night. Rain falling	9.3
5.30am 15th "	Stood to arms, then ordered stand by	(11)
3pm "	Marched to BAILLEUL to billets.	
5.30pm BAILLEUL	When getting into billets ordered parade at 7pm ready to move off.	
6.30pm "	Hour of parade postponed to 7.30pm	
7.30pm "	Paraded and marched off to STEENWERK.	
10pm STEENWERK	Halted and bivouacked in field W. of village.	
12 noon 16th "	17th and 18th Bdes across R. LYS. 19th Bde ordered to move at once to NEUVE-EGLISE, Battalion found advanced guard	(12)
1.30pm "	Entered BELGIUM	

Army Form C. 2118.

WAR DIARY
or
INTELLIGENCE SUMMARY.
(Erase heading not required.)

Instructions regarding War Diaries and Intelligence Summaries are contained in F.S. Regs., Part II. and the Staff Manual respectively. Title pages will be prepared in manuscript.

Hour, Date, Place	Summary of Events and Information	Remarks and references to Appendices
2 pm 16th October NEUVE-EGLISE	Ordered march on area KEMMEL – LA CLYTTE to VLAMERTINGHE	
7 pm " VLAMERTINGHE	"A" and "B" Coys took up outpost positions to cover town, the remainder of the Battalion moved into Billets. A cold, misty night.	M
10 am 17th "	Outpost Companies withdrawn to Billets.	M
6.30 am 18th "	Ordered to be ready to move at 30 minutes' notice.	M
10 am " "	Presbyterian Service.	
11.30 am " "	Practice Motor Bus Mort by the CAMERONIANS.	
1.45 pm 19th "	CAMERONIANS moved off in Motor Buses. Remainder of Bde marched off via LA CLYTTE – KEMMEL – NEUVE EGLISE [across BELGIAN frontier]	M 3 9
7.30 pm " "	onto Halted just across the frontier. Tea was cooked.	
9.15 pm " "	Moved on via STEENWERK – ESTAIRES to LAVENTIE. A wet night.	
2.30 am 20th " LAVENTIE	Battalion went into billets.	M
9 am " "	Ordered to parade at 12.30 pm to dig trenches.	
12 noon " "	Ordered parade at once to march to FROMELLES	
2 pm " " FROMELLES	Noted 1/Middlesex and 1/Royal Welsh Fusiliers took up line PONT-DE-PIERRE – FROMELLES. 2 Platoons "D" Coy (Lieut R.S.A.) took post on ridge W. of village. Battn bivouacked

WAR DIARY
of
INTELLIGENCE SUMMARY.
(Erase heading not required.)

Army Form C. 2118.

Hour, Date, Place		Summary of Events and Information	Remarks and references to Appendices
3.30 am	21st October, FROMELLES	Battalion paraded, the 2 Platoons "D" Coy being withdrawn, and marched to LE MAISNIL via PONT-DE-PIERRE	
4.15 am	" LE MAISNIL	Halted. French Cavalry were holding a line to the E and S of the village. "D" Coy put out posts on the roads running to the S and E and "B" Coy towards BADINGHEM. Patrols were found out from "B" and "D" Coys in first line, commenced to dig in on the line Section A – From a point 300 W of the LE MAISNIL – BAS FLANDRE road and about 300 stops from the cross roads in the village to the bottom of the V in VESPRES. "D" Coy Section B – From the V in VESPRES to a point just S of the B in BACQUART. "B" Coy "A" and "C" Coys, in Reserve, with 4 S.A.A. Carts, 1 Maltese Cart, and 1 Cooks Wagon, were placed in a field just W. of the Church. French Cavalry withdrew from S and SE without giving warning, but it was ascertained that 4 Squadrons remained to watch RADINGHEM, now reported clear of German troops	For Orders, message, reports see Appendix A Nos. 1 – 5. Sketch Plan of Ground Appendix B.
5.15 am	"		
6 am	"		

WAR DIARY
—or—
INTELLIGENCE SUMMARY.
(Erase heading not required.)

Army Form C. 2118.

Hour, Date, Place	Summary of Events and Information	Remarks and references to Appendices
6.15 am. 21st October LE MAISNIL	German Artillery shelled the village and continued throughout the action. 2 men of "A" Coy wounded by shrapnel	(M)
7 am.	Rifle fire heard from the direction of LA VOIRIE. "A" Coy brought up on right of Section A (D Coy) to fill up gap to 1/ROYAL WELSH FUSILIERS at PONT DE PIERRE as much as possible.	
9 am.	French reported that Cavalry had been driven out of RADINGHEM and their the Germans were advancing on LE MAISNIL. French Cavy. fell back on LA BOOTILLERIE leaving 100 Cyclists to guard the two LE MAISNIL — RADINGHEM roads. "C" Coy (Reserve) moved to about 300x to N.W. and transport horses to a farm ¼ mile N.W. of village, as shell fire very severe. Attack from S.E. developing and Lieut. LODER brought Machine Guns into action on left of Section A O.C. 1/MIDDLESEX Rgt., with 2 Companies, which he held in reserve near Battalion Reserve, arrived and took over command of the defence.	9 3
10 am.		
11 am.	Church steeple lettered	

Army Form C. 2118.

WAR DIARY
—or—
INTELLIGENCE SUMMARY.
(Erase heading not required.)

Instructions regarding War Diaries and Intelligence Summaries are contained in F.S. Regs., Part II. and the Staff Manual respectively. Title pages will be prepared in manuscript.

Hour, Date, Place	Summary of Events and Information	Remarks and references to Appendices
11.30 am 21st October LE MAISNIL	Hostile fire slackened. French officer & Cyclists arrived to take his men away but on receiving a request from G.O.C. 19th Infy Bde to hold his position consented to remain	(M)
12 noon " "	Capt. G. THORPE found and took over command of "A" Coy	
12.30 pm " "	Firing recommenced and became very severe, the house behind which the Machine Gun wagon was sheltering being struck, the horses bolting and the wagon upset, smashing the rear portion of	
2.7 pm	German Infantry attacked in force from E. French cyclists began to fall back without informing the O.C. defence.	
3 pm	As big gap still lay between the right of the defence and the ROYAL WELSH FUSILIERS. "A" Coy extended to endeavour to gain touch. Signs of an approaching attack against this line were evident. German attack from RADINGHEM along the 9 road very severe. "C" Coy ordered up to strengthen this flank, and also 1 Coy. 1/MIDDLESEX sent up. 2nd Lieut. BIRKIN killed while assisting 1 section of his platoon (B Coy) to cover position vacated by French cyclists. Machine	9 3 10.0

Army Form C. 2118.

WAR DIARY
or
INTELLIGENCE SUMMARY.
(Erase heading not required.)

Instructions regarding War Diaries and Intelligence Summaries are contained in F.S. Regs., Part II. and the Staff Manual respectively. Title pages will be prepared in manuscript.

Hour, Date, Place	Summary of Events and Information	Remarks and references to Appendices
3 pm. 21st October. LE MAISNIL	Guns moved to act against this attack	
4 pm. " "	Before Headquarters shelled, O.C. 1/MIDDLESEX escaping narrowly. Machine Guns withdrawn, one gun jammed and ammunition failing owing to letting of wagon.	
4.30 pm. " "	"C" Coy enfiladed by German Machine Gun and Rifle fire. CAPT. SANDEMAN 2/Lieuts. CAMPBELL (L.L.) FAIRBAIRN, and LOTHIAN (slightly) wounded and casualties very heavy. Last Platoon Coy ordered up.	
5 pm. " "	O.C. 1/MIDDLESEX severely wounded. CAPT. MOORHOUSE extricated the survivors of C. Coy and fell back to cross roads. 2 Coys CAMERONIANS reported to be coming up from BAS MAISNIL to support defence. Col. Moulton-Barrett ordered a general retirement towards BAS MAISNIL, informing O.C. ROYAL WELSH FUSILIERS. 2 Coys CAMERONIANS carried retirement.	
5.15 pm. " "		
5.30 pm. " "	Battalion reformed 500x N.W. of LE MAISNIL and took up a defensive line. Hostile artillery swept ground	
5.45 pm. " "	Retirement continued towards BAS MAISNIL. Many wounded had	

Army Form C. 2118.

WAR DIARY
or
INTELLIGENCE SUMMARY.
(Erase heading not required.)

Hour, Date, Place	Summary of Events and Information	Remarks and references to Appendices
5.45 p.m. 21st October LE MAISNIL	to be left, who could not walk, and three fell into German hands	
6 p.m. BAS MAISNIL	Remnt of the Battalion did not force on to the Battalion attacked	
" "	on to LA BOUTILLERIE to bivouac. Wounded taken over by	
" "	Ambulance. Transport had also to be abandoned.	
6.15 p.m. LA BOUTILLERIE	Bivouacked in field with 1/MIDDLESEX Regt. Capts URE & SANDEMAN,	
" "	Lieuts CAMPBELL (I.), FERRALIE, & BLACKLOCK and over 200 men missing.	
" "	1 Platoon A Coy (Lord ERSKINE, 2 Lieut) and 1 Platoon D Coy (2 Lieut AITKEN)	
" "	still to come in. "A" Coy (less 1 Platoon) took up a covering	
" "	position, in line with the CAMERONIANS and MIDDLESEX Regt, about	
" "	200 x to the front.	
10 p.m. "	Lieut Cocker AITKEN's Platoon (D Coy) marched in.	
12 midnight "	2 Lieut LORD ERSKINE's Platoon marched in.	
3.30 am 22nd "	1 Section "B" Coy came in, having lain in a trench, undiscovered	
" "	by the Germans, and made good their escape under cover of darkness	
5 am "	[failed to arr]	
5.40 am "	CAMERONIANS, MIDDLESEX and 1/ROYAL WELSH FUSILIERS to hold the	

WAR DIARY
or
INTELLIGENCE SUMMARY.

(Erase heading not required.)

Army Form C. 2118.

Hour, Date, Place	Summary of Events and Information	Remarks and references to Appendices
22nd October LA BOUTILLERIE	Line LE TOUQUET — ROUGES BANCS — CROIX BLANCHE. Battalion in reserve.	
5:40 am	Marched to ground about 200 N.W. of the R. of RUE DAVID and commenced to dig in. "B" and "D" Coys in first line, "A" and "C" Coys in second line.	
6 am		
6 pm	A German attack on the village was repulsed.	
	Men under cover. Heavy rifle fire in front.	
6:30 pm	Heavy cross.	
8 pm	Lieut. BUFT-MARSHAM and 1 Platoon ("A" Coy) marched out to act as escort to a Section 21st Batty. R.F.A. near ROUGE BANCS.	
OCT. 23rd		
4:30 am	Lieut. AITKEN and 1 Platoon ("D" Coy) marched out to act as escort to 42nd Batty. R.F.A. on the RUE PETILLON.	
5:30 am	Dugouts shelled. 4 Casualties.	
7 am	Horrible fire died down. "A" Coy ordered march to LE TOUQUET to support the left flank of the CAMERONIANS.	
2 pm	Heavy artillery fire. 3 Casualties.	
4 pm	Fire slackened.	
6:30 pm	"B", "C", & "D" Coys marched out from the dug-outs and bivouacked in a field.	

WAR DIARY
or
INTELLIGENCE SUMMARY.
(Erase heading not required.)

Army Form C. 2118.

Hour, Date, Place	Summary of Events and Information	Remarks and references to Appendices
6.30 pm. 23rd October, LA BOUTILLERIE, four S.E. of CROIX MARÉCHAL	The two Platoons were duly returned.	
5 am. 24th	Companies returned to the trenches.	
8 am. "	Lieut. BURT-MARSHALL and his Platoon opened and proceeded to "A"	
" "	Coy. Report of expected hostile attack so ammunition supply increased	
" "	Enemy's artillery shelled the line.	
10 am. "	Lieut. AITKEN and his Platoon returned.	
4.30 pm. "	Heavy firing heard from line of the 2nd Army Corps	2
6 pm. "	Firing spread to the 19th Bde, and the Artillery shelled heavily. The Battalion (less "A" Coy) marched up to the field (bivouack of the night 23rd-24th) and stood to.	3
7.30 pm. "	Firing died down. Men bivouacked for the night.	
10.30 pm. "	Outburst of firing which lasted ½ hour	
2 am. 26th	Firing broke out again but stopped quickly	
3.50 am. "	Another outburst of firing which stopped at 4.5 am	
5 am. "	Coys. returned to the dug-outs	
8 am. "	German Artillery fire opened and continued at intervals through the morning	

WAR DIARY
or
INTELLIGENCE SUMMARY.
(Erase heading not required.)

Army Form C. 2118.

Instructions regarding War Diaries and Intelligence Summaries are contained in F. S. Regs., Part II. and the Staff Manual respectively. Title pages will be prepared in manuscript.

Hour, Date, Place	Summary of Events and Information	Remarks and references to Appendices
2 pm 25th October LA BOUTILLERIE	Heavy shell fire on village	
5 pm "	Shelling stopped	
5.45 pm "	Coys came out from dug-outs and bivouacked in the field.	
10 pm "	Firing, commencing in the 2nd Army Corps, spread to the KRYAK WELSH FUSILIERS and 1/MIDDLESEX	(M)
11 pm "	Firing stopped	
5 am 26th "	Coys returned to the dug-outs.	
9 am "	Village shelled 19th / Bde. Hdqrs. moved to a farm 100 W. of CROIX MARÉCHAL cross roads	(M)
11 am "	G.O.C. 17th Inf. Bde. inspected ground immediately in rear of Battalion first line of dug-outs, in which 2 of two battalions were to dig a second line of defence	
2 pm "	Hostile shell fire recommenced	
5 pm "	All quiet. [Battalion (less 'A' Coy) ordered to bivouac in a field 200+ N. of CROIX MARÉCHAL cross roads.]	(M)
5 am 27th "	Coys marched back to the dug-outs.	

WAR DIARY
— OR —
INTELLIGENCE SUMMARY.
(Erase heading not required.)

Army Form C. 2118.

Instructions regarding War Diaries and Intelligence Summaries are contained in F.S. Regs., Part II. and the Staff Manual respectively. Title pages will be prepared in manuscript.

Hour, Date, Place	Summary of Events and Information	Remarks and references to Appendices
8.30 am 27th October. LA BOUTILLERIE	Occasional shelling by Germans	
5.30 pm " "	After a quiet afternoon marched up to bivouac in field near cross-roads.	
6 pm " "	"B" & "C" Coys went out to dig trenches in rear of ROYAL WELSH FUSILIERS.	
9.30 pm " "	Heavy firing in front. "B" and "C" Coys recalled	
10.30 pm " "	All quiet.	
11 pm " "	Firing recommenced. "D" Coy ordered to march to support "A" Coy as the Germans were reported to have occupied TOUQUET. "C" Coy guarding the CROIX-MARÉCHAL cross-roads and patrolling to LA BOUTILLERIE	
1.30 am 28th "	"C" and "D" Coys recalled. Report of German success proved false.	
5.15 am " "	Coys returned to dug-outs. Occasional shelling during morning	
5.30 pm " "	Coys marched up to bivouac.	
9 pm " "	"B" Coy and 20 men "C" Coy went out to dig trenches behind the ROYAL WELSH FUSILIERS	

WAR DIARY or INTELLIGENCE SUMMARY.

Army Form C. 2118.

(Erase heading not required.)

Instructions regarding War Diaries and Intelligence Summaries are contained in F.S. Regs., Part II. and the Staff Manual respectively. Title pages will be prepared in manuscript.

Hour, Date, Place	Summary of Events and Information	Remarks and references to Appendices
12 a.m. 27th October, LA BOUTILLERIE	Digging party returned	
1.50 a.m. 28th " "	Slow fight opened on Right of 19th Bde.	
3 a.m. " "	All quiet	
3.40 a.m. " "	Firing recommenced	
4.30 a.m. " "	All quiet	
5.15 a.m. " "	Coys returned to the dug outs	
9 a.m. " OCT 28th "	"D" Coy went out to construct dug out on left of and in continuation of "C" Coy	
3 p.m. " "	"D" Coy ceased work	
5 p.m. " "	2/Lieut CUNNINGHAM with 20 N.C.Os and men went out on permanent duty in rear of firing line hunting for enemy's snipers.	
5.30 p.m. " "	"B" Coy (60 men) and "C" Coy marched to continue digging line of trenches in rear of 'ROYAL WELSH FUSILIERS.' "D" Coy and "B" Coy (less 60 men) marched to bivouack	93
12 a.m. " "	Heavy firing in front. "B" and "C" Coys digging parties came in.	
2 a.m. 30th " "	"D" Coy ordered to take post at CROIX MARÉCHAL cross roads, with	

Army Form C. 2118.

WAR DIARY
or
INTELLIGENCE SUMMARY.
(Erase heading not required.)

Hour, Date, Place	Summary of Events and Information	Remarks and references to Appendices
2 a.m. 30th October. LA BOUTILLERE	1 Platoon 400ˣ down road towards village. "B" Coy moved to road junction just N. of the N in RUE PETILLON with 1 Platoon 400ˣ down the road running S.W. from the above road junction.	
2.30 a.m. " "	Germans reported to have broken the line of the 1/MIDDLESEX Regt. "D" Coy (Capt HENDERSON) ordered to march to support the MIDDLESEX, and "C" Coy (Capt MOORHOUSE) moved to field "D" Coy's first position.	
3.15 a.m. " "	Heavy outburst of firing. 1 Platoon "D" Coy (Lieut ROSE) went up to assist in driving out the Germans from a small nullah which they had occupied in their advance. 58 Germans killed and 12 wounded & captured, and nullah completely cleared.	nullah !
3.45 a.m. " "	"B" and "C" Coys returned to the Bivouac.	
4 a.m. " "	All quiet. Lieut CUNNINGHAM'S Sniper party recalled.	
5.30 a.m. " "	"D" Coy ordered to march back to dug-outs. Battalion marched down to dug-outs.	
6 a.m. " "	Heavy shelling commenced and continued till noon. 2/Lieut.	

WAR DIARY
OF
INTELLIGENCE SUMMARY.
(Erase heading not required.)

Army Form C. 2118.

Hour, Date, Place	Summary of Events and Information	Remarks and references to Appendices
6 am 30th October LA BOUTILLERIE	L.M. MACKINTOSH granted a Commission and posted to "C" Coy	(in)
4.30 pm "	Machine Gun detachment (Lieut LIDDELL) attached to ROYAL WELSH FUSILIERS and marched off to the trenches	
5.30 pm "	Battn. marched to bivouack in field	
10.30 pm "	Heavy firing in line of ROYAL WELSH FUSILIERS and 2nd Army Corps. German artillery shelled heavily	(in)
11.50 p.m "	All quiet	
2.10 am 31st	Firing broke out again and lasted for half an hour	
6 am "	Coys marched to dig outs	
10 pm "	"B" and "D" Coys went out to continue construction of Bombproofs in continuation of "C" Coys lines but were heavily shelled and had to stop.	9 3
5.30 pm "	Coys marched to the bivouack.	
6 pm "	30 men "B" Coy and "C" Coy went out to continue entrenching on rear of ROYAL WELSH FUSILIERS.	
11 pm "	Digging party returned	

WAR DIARY
or
INTELLIGENCE SUMMARY.
(Erase heading not required.)

Army Form C. 2118.

Hour, Date, Place	Summary of Events and Information	Remarks and references to Appendices
12 mn 28th–29th Ontside LA BOUTILLERIE	"A" Company (Capt THORPE) German attack expected. Have laid to meet attack in co-operation with Company CAMERONIANS (Capt RITCHIE)	(M)
2 am 29th " "	German attack. One Platoon (2/Lt STEWART) sent forward to the left front to support the CAMERONIANS. The attack strongly delivered 2/Lt ANDERSON, with 2 Platoon, coming up in support on the right, forced a German Machine Gun to cease fire.	(M)
4 am " "	Germans finally retired, leaving about 60 dead and 8 wounded. "A" Coy reformed and returned to the trenches.	
5.45 am " "	Firing continuous till daylight (5.45 am) Germans shelled twenty	

17th December, 1914

HHClark Lieut 29/12/14
2/Arg & Suth'd H'ds

SIGNALS.   Army Form C. 2121.

TO: 2/ A & S Highlanders

Day of Month: 21st   AAA

RADINGHEM is now held by the enemy. The 2nd Bn A and S Highlanders are moving at 3.30 am by FORMELLES and PONT DE PIERRE to LE MAESNIL to occupy that place.

At 7AM the 1st Bn Middlesex Rgt after its advanced companies have been relieved by a portion of the Royal Welch Fusiliers will concentrate immediately North of PONT DE PIERRE cross roads, and move thence to a point on the road immediately South of the B of BAS MAESNIL.

To enable the Middlesex Rgt to move as above indicated, the OC Royal Welch Fusiliers will re-arrange his present dispositions so that half battalion shall hold FROMELLES and the other half battalion PONT DE PIERRE, relieving the Middlesex companies in the latter place between 6.30 and 7AM.

"A" Form.   Army Form C. 2121.
MESSAGES AND SIGNALS   No. of Message

Prefix	Code	m.	Words	Charge	This message is on a/c of :	Rec'd. at	m.
Office of Origin and Service Instructions.			Sent			Date	
Page 22.			At	m.	Service.	From	A1.
			To			By	
			By	②	(Signature of "Franking Officer.")		

TO

Posts will be thrown forward to watch the roads leading to LE RIEZ and ~~LA VOIRIE~~ AAA LA VOIRIE and any other tracks leading towards the enemy. As soon as the Middlesex Regt has reached point on road under B of BAS MAISNIL, Bde HQ and 1st Cameronians will proceed via A of VERBANQUET to new position about ¼ mile SW of B of BAS MAISNIL

sd C P Heywood Capt.
B/M 19th Inf Bde.

From 19th INF BDE
Place
Time 2.45 AM.

MESSAGES AND SIGNALS. Army Form C. 2121.

Page 23

From A.2

TO: 19ᵗʰ INFY BDE

Sender's Number	Day of Month	In reply to Number	AAA
ASH 3	21/10/14		

Whole of French Cavalry from LA VOIRIE and BAS FLANDRE have been withdrawn and are concentrating at LA BOUTILLERIE AAA They report 4 Squadrons remaining on the LAD MAESNIL - EN - VESPRES and at 27 just N of 2nd S in VESPRES AAA This will necessitate my placing ½ Company on the Fromelle Roads the village is now being shelled from South

Over

From Lt A.L.S.H.
Place Le MAISNIL
Time 7.45 am

	Form.		Army Form C. 2121
C	**MESSAGES AND SIGNALS.**		No. of Message

Prefix	Code	m.	Words	Charge	This message is on a/c of:	Recd. at	m.
Office of Origin and Service Instructions.			Sent			Date	
Page 25			At	m.	5 Service.	From A4	
			To				
			By		(Signature of "Franking Officer.")	By	

TO —

| Sender's Number | Day of Month | In reply to Number | **AAA** |

In case of LE MAISNIL is to be held as long as at all possible but if obliged to retire by superior force the British Infantry under command of the Senior Officer will fall back in the direction of LA BOUTILLERIE, but retirement is only to be carried out in case of absolute necessity of which the Senior Officer on the spot will be the judge AAA Similar instructions have been given to Royal Welsh Fusiliers and their direction of retreat is similar to yours. Please acknowledge in writing.

From 19th Inf Bde
Place
Time 9-30 AM

MESSAGES AND SIGNALS.

Page 26

From A5

TO: A & S HQrs

Sender's Number: G 59
Day of Month: 21st
AAA

Your ASH 6 received AAA I do not always credit French reports and hope they may be wrong in this case AAA On hearing musketry fire in your direction ½ an hour ago I ordered Col Ward to take his battalion less two companies to reinforce LE MAISNIL AAA as senior officer, he will, on arrival of course assume command AAA Show him this message at once AAA also I have informed commandant of French artillery (ten guns) at FORMELLES that you were being shelled from BAS FLANDRE or vicinity and asked him to shell that neighbourhood

LE MAISNIL, 21st OCT. 1914.

Page 24.
Appendix B

Scale of Yards. (1 inch = 554.4 yds.) R.F. 1/20000

Enlargement from Ordnance Survey Map —
FRANCE Sheet 8 (LILLE) Scale 1/80,000.

British —
French —
German —

War Diary.

Hour, Date, Place.	Summary of Events and Information	Remarks and references to Appendices.

19th Infantry Brigade.

2nd BATTALION

ARGYLE & SUTHERLAND HIGHLANDERS

NOVEMBER 1914.

"Confidential."

121/2647

War Diary

of

2nd Bn. Argyll & Sutherland Highlanders.

19th Brigade

From 1st November 1914 to 30th November 1914.

(Volume IV)

Table of Contents

War Diary   Pages 1 to 7.

Appendices.

    A (Orders Received)   " 8 to 17.

    B (Sketch)   " 18

    C. (Messages)   " 19 to 21.

WAR DIARY
INTELLIGENCE SUMMARY

Army Form C. 2118.

Instructions regarding War Diaries and Intelligence Summaries are contained in F. S. Regs., Part II. and the Staff Manual respectively. Title pages will be prepared in manuscript.

(Erase heading not required.)

Hour, Date, Place	Summary of Events and Information	Remarks and references to Appendices
LA BOUTILLERIE 1st Nov.	Battalion ordered to march to ERGOINGHEM at about 12.30 p.m. A Company being relieved by Yorks and Lanc. Regiment. Batt. (B and A (6")) marched off at 2.30 had been ordered to ERGOIN GHEM, and then proceeded to dig trenches under orders of Bgd.r Gen.l GLUBB R.E. Machine gun section left with Middlesex Regt.	93
FARM between LA BOUTILLERIE 1st Nov. 5.45 p.m. and LE TOUQUET	A Company was relieved by co. of YORK and LANC. Regt. in their trenches, then marched to CROIX MARECHAL (Batt. H.Q.) and thence to join battalion at ERGOINGHEM, arriving 11 p.m.	
ERGOINGHEM 2nd Nov. 5 a.m.	A Co.y dig trenches in front of ERGOINGHEM (2nd line of defence)	
1 p.m.	Lt Col. Bonham Barrett gave up command of the Battalion, and his was temporarily taken by Captain H.B. HISLOP.	
4 p.m.	Battalion marched to PONT DE NIEPPE.	
PONT DE NIEPPE 3rd Nov. 9 a.m. to 4 p.m.	Carried out entrenchments on line LES TROIS TILLEULS — Windmill at W end of PONT DE NIEPPE.	
5 p.m.	Following officers joined battalion:- Major M.E. RODIE from 3rd Batt.n, Captains SOTHEBY, LESCHALLAS and HEYS THOMSON from 4th Batt.	
4th Nov.	Work on entrenchments continued as for 3rd.	
5th "	do	
6th "	do	
"	Major H.B. Kirk arrived and took over command of battalion.	
7th " 9 a.m.	Orders received from 3rd Corps to do no work today as you will be required to work elsewhere tonight. Capt HYSLOP and Lt BURT MARSHALL sent to reconnoitre portion to be entrenched.	
" 11 a.m.		
PONT DE NIEPPE 12 noon	General Staff officer from 4th Div visited Batt.n H.Q. and requested that the Batt.n be prepared to move at short notice so as to support 4th Div if required.	

2

WAR DIARY
or
INTELLIGENCE SUMMARY
(Erase heading not required.)

Army Form C. 2118.

Hour, Date, Place		Summary of Events and Information	Remarks and references to Appendices
PONT DE NIEPPE 7th Nov (cont.)	1.30 p.m.	Orders received from 4th Div. to move to LE BIZET sending officer to 11th Bde H.Qrs for orders.	9.3 a.m.
	2 p.m.	Marched off, adjutant sent to 11th Bde H.Q. Brig Gen HUNTER WESTON ordered battalion to move to PLOEGSTEERT	
LE BIZET	3 p.m.	Marched on to PLOEGSTEERT and reported to Lt Col BUTLER. Went into bivouac in some field W of village.	
PLOEGSTEERT	4.20 p.m.	Order from Lt Col BUTLER to move one Cov to report to O.C. HANTS Regt ¾ mile East of PLOEGSTEERT. D company (Capt W.A. HENDERSON) sent.	Order marked Appendix A 1.
	4.30 p.m. 4.50 p.m.	C Company sent under orders of Lt Col A.L. HINGSFOLIOT? (Capt MOORHOUSE) to move battalion via TOUQUET to LE BIZET to support Rifle Bde. Marched there. Ordered to move battalion to TOUQUET via LE BIZET to support Rifle Bde. Marched there.	
TOUQUET		and found that KING'S OWN regiment was due to arrive alone. Waited till they arrived.	
PLOEGSTEERT	7 p.m. 9 p.m.	Marched back to PLOEGSTEERT. Bivouacked North of PLOEGSTEERT. Lieut ROSE wounded.	
PLOEGSTEERT 8th Nov.	5 a.m.	Moved battalion (less D and C Coys and machine gun section) into billets in PLOEGSTEERT WOOD	
	3 p.m.	Informed that battalion would take up trenches in PLOEGSTEERT WOOD	
	5.30 p.m.	D Company rejoined battalion but left Lt AITKEN with one platoon with HANTS regt. Moved into PLOEGSTEERT WOOD to take up position in front line. A very muddy walk, relief not completed till 11 p.m. B company left over from right to central path through wood, A company prolonging on left to join up with Lanc Fusiliers. Battalion warned that attack next day by Hon. is probable.	Order marked Appendix A 2
PLOEGSTEERT WOOD 9th Nov		Spent a good morning in trenches	
	12 noon	B Co.'s confirmed that on lyddite shells were coming on their trenches. Capt SOTHEBY wounded by our shrapnel.	
	1 p.m.	Orders received that ½ German force on line will be attacked that night, any 11 and Scottish Highlanders making attack. Reconnaissance must therefore be carried out as far as possible. Lieut MACPHERSON and one German howitzer shelled B Company trenches. 11 men wounded.	Order marked Appendix A 3.

Army Form C. 2118.

WAR DIARY
INTELLIGENCE SUMMARY.
(Erase heading not required.)

Instructions regarding War Diaries and Intelligence Summaries are contained in F.S. Regs., Part II. and the Staff Manual respectively. Title pages will be prepared in manuscript.

Hour, Date, Place		Summary of Events and Information	Remarks and references to Appendices
PLOEGSTEERT WOOD	9th Nov. 2 p.m.	Order from Col. BUTLER arrange for conference between C.O.'s units concerned at 2.30 p.m. at A.S.H. H.Q.s to arrange details of night attack.	Map of PLOEGSTEERT WOOD marked Appendix B
"	2.30 p.m. to 3 p.m.	Reconnaissance carried out by 2nd Lieut Cunningham and by Major Sergt CAMPBELL.	
"	3 p.m.	2nd Lieut CUNNINGHAM reports that Eastern edge of wood has a road along it. The road hedge is passable, but the hedge on the far side of the road is up a bank and very thick and forms a very difficult obstacle.	
"	"	Sergt CAMPBELL reports that the enemy are holding a trench at right angles to the edge of the wood, facing North. A deep wet ditch would delay an advance against the Western end of the trench from the wood.	
"	3.40 p.m.	Conference held to discuss attack.— Present Lt. Col. Butler commanding PLOEGSTEERT WOOD Section, Major H.B.KIRK commanding 2nd A and S. Hdrs, Major PROVSE, commanding S.O.M.I.I, Lt Col Cunningham East Lancs, Capt WOODMAN, comdg Lanc. Fus. It was agreed that attack should take place at 11.30 p.m., preceded by ½ hour's bombardment. Three selected M.G. guns to rack beginning and end of the bombardment. The East Lancs were the to move North from LE GHEER and seize the German trenches between that point and just marked A on map. ½ B Coy. was to advance East to the edge of the wood South of the manrinele and occupy the attention of the land just clear of the wood. A company and D company were to debouch from the wood by the right tunnel of Lane Fms and then A company were to attack the trenches about the quadrangle marked B and D company the quadrangle trench marked C. The line of the bombardment was to be until to get as close as possible, and when the bombardment ceased at 11.30 p.m. the assault was to be delivered. ½ B Coy. was to support D company.	Order marked Appendix A 4.
"	9.30 p.m.	Front trenches taken over by Lanc. Fus. Our artillery kept up desultory fire.	
"	10 p.m.	D company moved out to position, followed by A company and ½ B company	
"	11 p.m.	Heavy bombardment by artillery commences. This sets fire to house marked D on sketch.	

Army Form C. 2118.

WAR DIARY
INTELLIGENCE SUMMARY.
(Erase heading not required.)

Instructions regarding War Diaries and Intelligence Summaries are contained in F. S. Regs., Part II. and the Staff Manual respectively. Title pages will be prepared in manuscript.

Hour, Date, Place		Summary of Events and Information	Remarks and references to Appendices
PLOEGSTEERT WOOD	9th Nov. 11.30 p.m.	Bombardment ceased. ½ B Coy advanced up to edge of wood, which they reached without being fired at. A and D coys were then between the ST YVES - LE GHEER road and the edge of the wood, behind the Lone Fur. French, and with them began to advance.	
	11.45 p.m.	D Company's objective was the N.W. angle of guardangle C. Officer arriving at the burning house (D) Capt. W. A. HENDERSON gave the order to charge but was at once hit and fell. A Company was meanwhile working through the houses just East of the wood.	
		D Company then unfortunately lost direction and with A Company closed to attack quadrangle B. This attack therefore was subjected to heavy enfilade fire from the Eastern face of quadrangle C and though it penetrated and cut the wire in front of the hedge at B, failed.	
10th Nov.	12.30 a.m.	Lieut CLARK with ½ B Coy was in support of D Coy and behind its left. When the first attack failed, he collected men from A and D coys and with that and his half company led them round the burning house and again tried to attack the trenches about B.	
	2 a.m.	The enemy in the meantime had brought up reinforcements and there from C were threatening the road about CLARK'S attack. This attack had been subject to machine gun fire from B and C, and eventually retired to the trenches evacuated by A Company.	
9th Nov.	12 m.n.	½ B Co (Major ROUSE), having reached the edge of the wood, was found that in places the artillery had broken down the hedge in front of the German trenches, and tried to charge these. This attack was at once met by a very heavy fire and could not get past the hedge. The ½ Coy to which I could not be crossed. The enemy was made two efforts to charge the trenches but This ½ Coy was ordered to retire. Captain HYSOP got out to bring them back.	
10th Nov.	3 a.m.		
	4.30 a.m.	The battalion was ordered to take up a position in the support trenches in the wood. The casualties in this action consisted of 3 Officers missing Capt W.A. HENDERSON Lieut W BORT MARSHALL and 2nd Lieut FETHERSTONHAUGH, one officer slightly wounded (2nd Lieut BUCHANAN) other ranks 10 killed 91 wounded 45 missing. Their casualties were out of only about 330 men engaged.	

Forms/C. 2118/11

WAR DIARY
INTELLIGENCE SUMMARY

Army Form C. 2118.

Hour, Date, Place		Summary of Events and Information	Remarks and references to Appendices
PLOEGSTEERT WOOD	10th Nov. 4.30 a.m.	The wounded had been brought back to the trenches originally held by the Battalion, and were now carried further back. A number could however not be found.	
"	" 6.30 a.m.	Battalion in position in support trenches. B Coy ordered to front line between Lan Fus and East Lancs.	G.2.
"	" 7 a.m.	Orders received to strengthen line as far as possible.	
"	" 11.30 a.m.	Congratulatory message received from Major Genl commanding 11th Inf Bde containing message from C. in C.	Marked Appendix C.1.
"	" 8.30 p.m.	Carried out work strengthening 2nd line in wood. B Coy heavily shelled in front trenches. Congratulatory message from Genrl Gordon Con. in 19th Bde.	Marked Appendix C.2.
"	11th Nov. 12 noon	D Company relieved B Coy in firing line. Message received from Genrl Kerr 6th Div to take over the front of line at 5 a.m. Arranged with East Lan and Lan Fus to	" C.3.
"	" 5.30 p.m.	Ordered to withdraw D Coy from firing line.	
"	" 11.50 p.m.	Ordered to send one company to report to Som L.I. for work on intrenchments. A Coy sent. This company received orders to dig all night, ½ coy to intrenchments with Somersets, ½ coy to return to wood before dawn.	
"	12th Nov. 5.30 a.m.	Reliefs of D Coy carried out.	
"	" 5 a.m.	½ A Coy (2nd Lieut STEWART) went into shelters near Som L.I. (STYVES) and	
"	" 10 a.m.	were heavily shelled 4 casualties.	
"	" 6 p.m.	Continued work all day strengthening 2nd line. Orders received to concentrate Battalion at PLOEGSTEERT next morning, and then march to BAC ST MAUR. ½ A Coy to be relieved at night by Worcesters and then rejoin. Orders issued to concentrate at mill West of PLOEGSTEERT at 8 a.m.	Appendix A.5.
MILL PLOEGSTEERT	13th Nov 6.15 a.m.	Moved off from PLOEGSTEERT WOOD. (First lot since entering the WOOD).	
"	" 8 a.m.	Breakfasts.	

6.

Army Form C. 2118.

WAR DIARY
or
~~INTELLIGENCE SUMMARY~~
(Erase heading not required.)

Instructions regarding War Diaries and Intelligence Summaries are contained in F.S. Regs., Part II. and the Staff Manual respectively. Title pages will be prepared in manuscript.

Place	Hour, Date		Summary of Events and Information	Remarks and references to Appendices
PLOEGSTEERT	13th Nov	10 a.m.	Marched off. Received orders to rejoin 19th Bde.	
RUE BATAILLE	" "	1 p.m.	Went into billets.	
"	" 14th "		In billets all day. 19th Bde were relieved from trenches, but our machine gun	93 R.F.
"	" 15th "		Section remained with 20th R.B.	
"	" 16th "		In billets. Lieut Hd qrs B PURVES rejoined with draft of 97 men.	
"	" " "		" " Lieut LIDDELL and M.G. Section relieved from trenches and rejoined battalion. Capt MOORHOUSE sent to see trenches that he is to take over next day.	
"	" 17th "	10 a.m.	Warning order received that battalion will move that afternoon.	
"	" " "	1.15 p.m.	Orders to move at 2.40 p.m.	
"	" " "	2.40 p.m.	Marched off, halted outside ARMENTIERES for teas, and marched on to HOUPLINES.	
HOUPLINES	" "	5.30 to 9.30 p.m.	Took over trenches from R. Warwicks and R. Dub. Fusiliers. B, C, D and ½ A in front line. ½ A in reserve.	
"	18th Nov.		In trenches. Commenced work connecting up trenches.	
"	19th "		" Snow and hard frost. Continued work, wire entanglements made.	
"	20th "		" Improvements to trenches. Hard frost.	
"	21st "		" Draft of 150 men under Capt KENNEDY and Lieut HUTCHISON arrived. Hard frost. Farm of PONT BALLOT set on fire by enemy's shells.	
"	22nd "		In trenches. Worried by snipers. Officers visited M.G. and a machine gun was	
"	23rd "		Shelled by howitzers. Draft went to join companies. Arranged to keep 1 platoon per co's out of trenches in billets, giving each platoon 2 days rest. Draft of 52 men joined.	
"	24th "		In trenches. Work continued. Turned in field a night of PONT BALLOT farm. Lt Lieut BOYD joined.	
			Commenced. Commenced plan from farms opposite trenches. Sniping bad from farms opposite trenches.	

WAR DIARY
INTELLIGENCE SUMMARY
(Erase heading not required.)

Army Form C. 2118.

Instructions regarding War Diaries and Intelligence Summaries are contained in F.S. Regs., Part II. and the Staff Manual respectively. Title pages will be prepared in manuscript.

Hour, Date, Place		Summary of Events and Information	Remarks and references to Appendices
HOUPLINES	25th Nov. 12 noon	Howitzers shelled house in front of A Coy. Bolted about 20 Germans. Found range of these houses and German trench.	
"	26th Nov.	In trenches. Quiet day. Work proceeded with well. Officers and section Commanders of incoming 5th S.R. came into trenches to learn duties.	93rd
"	27th Nov. 2 a.m.	In trenches. Enemy shelled new trench on right of PONT BALLOT road. This was then unoccupied. Snipers active against C Coy and B Coy.	
"	28th 5 a.m.	Search light and rifle fire interrupted work in front of PONT BALLOT.	
	5 p.m.	Sniping bad again – B Coy. Major ROUSE wounded. One Coy (10 men) of 5th S.R. took over our trenches. Detachment charged across left flank of D, B and C Coys.	
"	29th	In trenches. Heavy fire from enemy in opposition against our aeroplane.	
	5 p.m.	A Coy sent out covering party (Capt HEYS THOMPSON) to cover R.E. blowing up farm opposite their trenches.	
	9 p.m.	Farm satisfactorily blown up. A second Coy of 5th S.R. relieved the first.	
	30th	In trenches. New machine gun emplacement made on PONT BALLOT road.	

"A" Form. Army Form C. 2121.
MESSAGES AND SIGNALS.
No. of Message 8.

Prefix	Code	m.	Words	Charge		This message is on a/c of:	Recd. at	m.
Office of Origin and Service Instructions.			Sent				Date	8
			At	m.		Service.	From	
			To					
			By			(Signature of "Franking Officer.")	By	

TO { Appendix A. 1

| Sender's Number | Day of Month | In reply to Number | |
| BA 35. | 7" | | AAA |

Situation 3.30 p.m: Germans still in position west of square L 7. AAA. INNIS FUS and WORCESTERS have reached the east end of PLOEGSTEERT wood AAA. E. LANCS have been sent up to North of LE GHEER and in cooperation with INNIS FUS have been directed to attack and restore the line at all costs. AAA. WORCESTERS, HANTS and SOM L I. to cooperate as may be possible without leaving forward line of trenches AAA. O.C. A & S Highlanders will send one company at once to report at H Q HANTS REGT ¾ mile east of PLOEGSTEERT cross roads on the LE GHEER road as a reserve under the orders of O.C. HANTS

From
Place
Time

The above may be forwarded as now corrected.   (2)

Censor. Signature of Addressor or person authorised to telegraph in his name
*This line should be erased if not required.

"A" Form.   Army Form C. 2121.
MESSAGES AND SIGNALS.   No. of Message 9

Prefix	Code	m.	Words	Charge	This message is on a/c of :	Recd. at	m
Office of Origin and Service Instructions			Sent At m. To By		Service. (Signature of "Franking Officer.")	Date 9 From By	

TO   Appendix A 1

Sender's Number	Day of Month	In reply to Number	AAA
BA 35.	7.		

Remainder of A & S Highlanders to remain in reserve in close billets north of PLOEGSTEERT sending two orderlies to Col BUTLERS H.Q. at 9th MILESTONE AAA. O.C. LAN. FUS will place one Coy on the road by the CHAU as a reserve on the MESSINES road the Remainder of battalion to remain in present position South west of Point 63 AAA. Garrison ~~have left centre~~ DORSETS. SOM.L.I. and HANTS will remain in their present position AAA. ~~WARW~~ FUS Coy will also remain in its present position AAA. Once the situation is fully restored and the original line made good the E. LANCS will occupy and hold the Sub-section north of LE GHEER relieving the WORCESTR

From		
Place		
Time		

"A" Form. Army Form C. 2121.
MESSAGES AND SIGNALS.

| TO | Appendix A | 1 |

| Sender's Number | Day of Month | In reply to Number | |
| 3435 | 7 | | AAA |

who will concentrate in reserve north of the last T of PLOEGSTEERT after being properly relieved arrangements for which will be made direct by OC WORCESTERS and E. LANCS. AAA. Similarly when the line has been restored and the relief of the WORCESTERS by the E. LANCS completed the INNIS FUS will reoccupy the trenches in the second line which they have been holding.

From Lt Col BUTLER
Time 4-2 pm.

D. Ovey Capt

"A" Form.
Army Form C. 2121.
MESSAGES AND SIGNALS. No 11

Prefix	Code	m.	Words	Charge	This message is on a/c of:	Recd. at	m.
Office of Origin and Service Instructions		Sent			Service.	Date	11
		At	m.			From	
		To				By	
		By		(Signature of "Franking Officer.")		

TO: Appendix A 2

| Sender's Number | Day of Month | In reply to Number | AAA |
| BC 26 | 8th | | |

Dispositions tonight.

(1) DORSET REGT and SOM.L.I. and HANTS will remain in occupation of their present positions AAA (2) E LANCS will relieve the Coy WORCESTER REGT now in their trenches and will continue to hold their present dispositions AAA

(3) The ARGYLL & SUTHERLAND HIGHLANDERS (less 1 Coy) will relieve that portion of the SEAFORTH HIGHLANDERS WORCESTERS and INNIS FUS occupying the front line from the left of the E.LANCS to the right of the left (B) company of the INNIS FUS AAA arrangements will be made direct between O. Commanding concerned.

(4) The LAN FUS will relieve with two coys the left (B) Coy INNIS FUS and such portions of other units

From
Place
Time

The above may be forwarded as now corrected (Z)

Censor. Signature of Addressor or person authorised to telegraph in his name

*This line should be erased if not required.

"A" Form.   Army Form C. 2121.
MESSAGES AND SIGNALS.   12   No of Message

Prefix	Code	m.	Words	Charge	This message is on a/c of		Recd. at	m.
Office of Origin and Service Instructions				Sent	Service.		Date	12
			At	m.			From	
			To		(Signature of "Franking Officer.")		By	
			By					

TO   Appendix A (2)

| Sender's Number | Day of Month | In reply to Number | AAA |
| BC 26 | 8 | | |

as are in front and line of trenches between
that Company and the right of the
IRISH FUS AAA The remaining half Battalion
will relieve that portion of the INNIS FUS
in the supporting trenches in PLOEGSTEERT
WOOD AAA.

(5) R.I. Fus Company will not be relieved and
will come under the orders of Major PRIMROSE
Commanding SOMERSETS AAA

(6) When relieved the INNIS FUS and Company
SEAFORTHS will move into close billets
East of PLOEGSTEERT on the PLOEGSTEERT –
LE GHEER road AAA The WORCESTERS
to close billet west of the PLOEGSTEERT –
MESSINES road North of PLOEGSTEERT AAA
Position of H.Q to be notified AAA.

(7) The Royal Scot Fus will relieve C Coy LAN FUS

From
Place
Time

"A" Form.   Army Form C. 2121.
MESSAGES AND SIGNALS.   No. of Message 13

Prefix	Code	m.	Words	Charge	This message is on a/c of:	Recd. at	m.
Office of Origin and Service Instructions.			Sent			Date	
			At	m.	Service.	From	13
			To				
			By		(Signature of "Franking Officer.")	By	

TO Appendix A 2

| Sender's Number | Day of Month | In reply to Number | AAA |

BC 26   8th

~~the~~ as a reserve on the MESSINES road South of the CHAV AAA.
(8) BEDFORD REGT will relieve the LAN FUS on the PETIT POINT road South of POINT 63 in reserve AAA.
(9) One company ARGYLL & S.H. and 1 platoon LAN FUS will remain holding the approaches to the second line trenches AAA.
(10) The 2nd WILTS REGT will relieve one coy ARGYLL & S.H. on the PLOEGSTEERT – LE GHEER road at the H.Q. of the HANTS AAA.

From
Place LT COL BUTLER.   D. Ovey
Time   9th MILESTONE

The above may be forwarded as now corrected.   (Z)

Censor.   Signature of Addressor or person authorised to telegraph in his name

"A" Form.
Army Form C. 2121.

MESSAGES AND SIGNALS.

No of Message 14

| Prefix | Code | m. | Words | Charge | This message is on a/c of: | Recd. at | m. |
Office of Origin and Service Instructions

Sent

At Appendix A m. 3. Service. Date 14
To From
By (Signature of "Franking Officer.") By

TO ARGYLL & S. H.

Sender's Number: BC2
Day of Month: 9
In reply to Number:

AAA

With reference to the proposed attack tonight with the object of restoring the line AAA. The attack will be made by the Argyll & S.H. supported by the LAN. FUS AAA. As the ARGYLL & S.H. advance their place will be taken by the reserve companies of the LAN.FUS and as soon as the original line of trenches has been secured the LAN.FUS will advance, occupy the trenches and dig in covered by the ARGYLL & S.H. AAA. As soon as the LAN.FUS have established themselves on the line regained the A & S.H. will fall back and reform at the supporting trenches in PLOEGSTEERT WOOD AAA. The O.C. LAN.FUS and A & S.H will confer with each other and MAJOR PROWSE commanding the S.L.I. with regard to the details of the attack and mutual cooperation AAA. All possible reconnaissances will be carried out and all arrangements for facilitating the

From LT. COL BUTLER
Place
Time

The above may be forwarded as now corrected (Z)

Censor. Signature of Addressor or person authorised to telegraph in his name
*This line should be erased if not required.

"A" Form. Army Form C. 2121.

MESSAGES AND SIGNALS.

TO: Appendix A 3

Sender's Number: BC.2
Day of Month: 9th
AAA

attack made such as cutting wire etc: AAA.
Please report whether any additional light
pistols, grenades, cutting tools etc are
required.

D. Oxey Capt.

From: LT. COL BUTLER.
Time: 10.3. am.

MESSAGES AND SIGNALS.

No. of Message **16**

From **16**

TO ARGYLL & S.H.   Appendix A(4)

Sender's Number **BC 14**   Day of Month **NINTH**   AAA

1A/ DISPOSITIONS TONIGHT :—
DORSET REGT — SOM LI — IRISH FUS retain present positions in Trenches

1B/ WILTS REGT will remain in Support within PLOEGSTEERT - LE GHEER Road under the orders of O.C. HANTS REGT

1C/ The following units will remain in reserve and will stand to arms as follows — all at 4 pm tonight. WORCS REGT head at 9th Milestone. Coy SEAFORTHS to JOIN WORCS REGT and act under orders of Offr Cmdg. INNISKILLING FUS one company at hd qrs of supporting companies in PLOEGSTEERT WOOD remainder of Battn head at junction of ride leading to above Hd Qrs and the second line of Trenches by the Barbed wire gate

MESSAGES AND SIGNALS.

Appendix A 4

BC 14

BEDFORD REGT head at CHAU on the MESSINES Road

YORKSHIRE REGT head at crossroads at PLOEGSTEERT

2) a. The following units will cooperate in an attack on the GERMANS about the KINK in the road under instructions which have been issued direct to OCs concerned LANC FUS — A & S HIGHRS and E LANCS

2 b) The SCOTS FUS will remain in support in the PLOEGSTEERT wood under the orders of LT COL BUTLER

3) HQrs COL BUTLER behind supporting trenches in PLOEGSTEERT WOOD [present headquarters of A & S H]

HQrs 11th Brig at 9th Milestone from 10 pm this evening

From LT COL BUTLER
Time 8.5 pm

Appendix B

Ploegsteert Wood – November 8th – 13th.

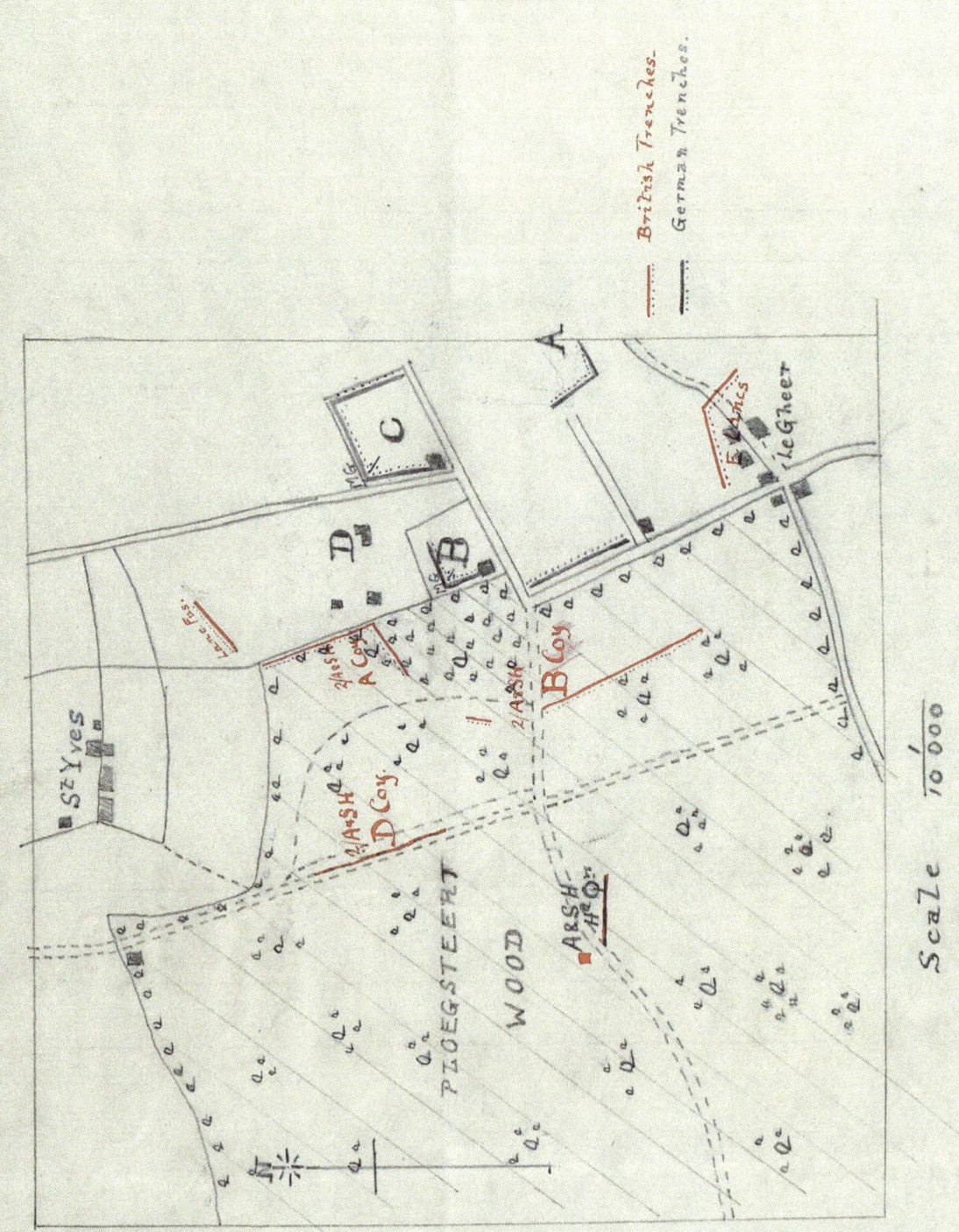

Appendix C

"C" Form (Duplicate).   Army Form C. 2123.
MESSAGES AND SIGNALS.   No. of Message **20**

| Charges to Pay. | Office Stamp. |
| £   s.   d. | **20** |

Service Instructions.

Handed in at the _____ Office, at _____ m. Received here at _____ m.

TO   **ARGYLL AND S. HIGHLANDERS**

| Sender's Number. | Day of Month. | In reply to Number. | |
| B16 | 10TH | | AAA |

The following message received from General GORDON Cmdg 19TH Inf Brigade Begins please convey following message to Argyll and Sutherland Highlanders AAA General GORDON and your comrades of 19TH Inf Brigade are proud to hear of your gallant work ends

FROM   COL BUTLER
PLACE
TIME   7.5 PM

Appendix C1. "C" Form (Original). 19 Army Form C. 2123.
MESSAGES AND SIGNALS. No. of Message ____

Prefix	Code	Words	Received	Sent, or sent out	Office Stamp.
£ s. d.			From	At ____ m.	19
Charges to collect			By	To	
Service Instructions.				By	

Two addresses

Handed in at the _____ Office, at _____ m. Received here at _____ m.

TO ARGYLLS LANC FUS

Sender's Number.	Day of Month.	In reply to Number.	
BM 28	Tenth	—	AAA

congratulations on your excellent
work last night AAA with
a little luck you ~~could~~ would have
achieved a great success the
commander in Chief wires to say
you have done very well

FROM   ELEVENTH INF BRIG
PLACE
TIME   10.50 AM

MESSAGES AND SIGNALS. Army Form C. 2123.

No. of Message 21

Prefix ___ Words ___

Charges to collect ___

Service Instructions: Apparent

Received From C3 By ___

Sent, or sent out At ___ m. To ___ By ___

Office Stamp. 21

Handed in at the ___ Office, at ___ m. Received here at ___ m.

TO: **A. AND S. HIGHLANDERS**

Sender's Number.	Day of Month.	In reply to Number.	AAA
BA23	11th		

Following message received from 6th Division begins please convey to A and S HIGHLANDERS general KIERS congratulations on very good work performed by the battalion in last nights operations ends message turned 9.30 AM yesterday

FROM: COL BUTLER
PLACE:
TIME: 10.17 M

19th Infantry Brigade.

2 DIV / 1365.

2nd BATTALION

ARGYLE & SUTHERLAND HIGHLANDERS

DECEMBER 1914.

121/3889

Confidential.

War Diary.

— of — 19th Brigade.

2nd Battalion, Argyll & Sutherland Highlanders.

From 1st December 1914 to 31st December, 1914.

(Volume 5.)

Index.

	Pages.
Summary of Events	1 to 7.
Appendix A1.	8.
Appendix B1.	9.

WAR DIARY
INTELLIGENCE SUMMARY

Army Form C. 2118.

Instructions regarding War Diaries and Intelligence Summaries are contained in F.S. Regs., Part II. and the Staff Manual respectively. Title pages will be prepared in manuscript.

(Erase heading not required.)

Place	Hour, Date	Summary of Events and Information	Remarks and references to Appendices
HOOPLINES	1st Dec.	In trenches. The thaw after the hard frost had caused a lot of damage to the trenches, and a great deal of repair work had to be done.	
"	6 p.m.	Sergt 6th Dr. Dixon received on recovering His Majesty THE KING'S visit.	Marked Appendix A1.
	2nd Dec. 10.30 a.m.	Lieut AITKEN, No 693 C.S.M. MARKEY, 9696 Sergt COULIE, 7423 Sergt SWAN, 9470 Cpl MULLEN, 506 L/Cpl BELL, 7443 L/Cpl COWAN, 8457 Pte KENNEDY and No 4570 Pte BENSON marched to CROIX DO BAC to represent the Battalion at His Majesty's Inspection. After the inspection His Majesty presented the Distinguished Conduct medal to No 9947 Sergt R. Ross for gallant conduct during the action at LE MAISNIL.	9³...
	3rd Dec.	In trenches. D Company erected new wire entanglements.	[6] [5]
	4th Dec.	In trenches.	
	2.30 p.m.	Enemy commenced shelling vicinity of Battn Head Quarters. About 12 shells were fired, falling in the houses in the immediate vicinity.	
	2.45 p.m.	Enemy directed artillery fire against farm occupied by three platoons of D Coy. Three men were wounded and it was decided to change their billets.	
	3 p.m.	High explosive shells were turned on to the neighborhood of the farm, but the company was moved without further casualties.	[6]
	5th Dec.	In trenches. Quiet day. WE caused further damage to trenches.	[5]

(9-29-6) W 2794 100,000 9/14 H W V Forms/C. 2118/11

2/

WAR DIARY
INTELLIGENCE SUMMARY.
(Erase heading not required.)

Army Form C. 2118.

Instructions regarding War Diaries and Intelligence Summaries are contained in F.S. Regs., Part II. and the Staff Manual respectively. Title pages will be prepared in manuscript.

Hour, Date, Place		Summary of Events and Information	Remarks and references to Appendices
HOUPLINES	6th Dec.	In trenches.	
	11.30 a.m.	Enemy commenced shelling neighbourhood of Battn. Hd. Qrs. Three platoons billetted in school close by had to be moved to safer billets. About 30 shells were fired by the enemy.	
		No casualties, but 2 civilians in neighbouring house killed.	
"	7th Dec.	In trenches. Very wet day. Rain did a lot of damage to trenches, owing to parapets and traverses being washed away.	[5]
"		Draft of 204 men under 2nd Lieuts MOIR and LYLE arrived.	[5]
8th Dec.		In trenches. Work at repairing trenches.	[5]
9th Dec.		In trenches.	
"		"	9.3—
"	3.30 p.m.	Draft of 20 men [under 2nd Lieut BANKIER] arrived. This officer had orders to return next day	
"	5 p.m.	80 men of draft of 7th Dec. went out to dig supporting trench behind PONT BALLOT.	
"	7.30 p.m.	Enemy opened machine gun fire against trench occupied by A Coy. and advanced up to within 150 yards of this trench.	
"	9.35 p.m.	Enemy opened artillery fire, searching rear of trenches. An artillery guard and attack steamed off towards trenches held by 5th Scottish Rifles (1 Coy.) attached to batt. and Middlesex Regt. on our left. O few men advanced against B Coy	

(9 29 6) W 2794 100,000 9/14 H W V   Forms/C. 2118/11

Army Form C. 2118.

WAR DIARY
or
INTELLIGENCE SUMMARY.
(Erase heading not required.)

Instructions regarding War Diaries and Intelligence Summaries are contained in F. S. Regs., Part II. and the Staff Manual respectively. Title pages will be prepared in manuscript.

Hour, Date, Place		Summary of Events and Information	Remarks and references to Appendices
HOUPLINES	9th Dec.	Artson retired. Counter attack.	
"	"	8 p.m.	Enemy opened artillery fire on Trenches, shrapnel and high explosive. Casualties during ad'n 3 men Scottish Rifles killed, 5 men 2nd A.&S.H. wounded. Enemy's loss unknown.	
"	10th Dec.		Quiet day in trenches. Some wire found to be cut by shell fire and parapet broken in places.	Report attached marked Appendix B 1.
"	"	5 p.m.	All D Coy went into trenches, taking over their own part of the line and two platoons relieving the company of 5th Scottish Rifles on our left.	
"	"	11 p.m.	Orders received that Cameronians are to relieve battalion in trenches on night of 11th.	(a)
"	11th Dec.	8 a.m.	Orders received that after relief by Cameronians battalion is to go into Divnl Reserve at LUNATIC ASYLUM ARMENTIERES.	
"	"	10 a.m.	C. O. & Qrt A. & S. H.rs and Cameronians arrange details of relief.	
"	"	5 p.m.	Cameronians began relief of our trenches. Very wet night.	
"	"	9 p.m.	Relief completed. Het Bn moved off from HOUPLINES with last platoon to be relieved.	
"	"	10 p.m.	Whole battalion billetted.	(c)

LUNATIC ASYLUM
ARMENTIERES

Army Form C. 2118.

WAR DIARY
or
INTELLIGENCE SUMMARY.
(Erase heading not required.)

Instructions regarding War Diaries and Intelligence Summaries are contained in F.S. Regs., Part II. and the Staff Manual respectively. Title pages will be prepared in manuscript.

Hour, Date, Place		Summary of Events and Information	Remarks and references to Appendices
LUNATIC ASYLUM ARMENTIERES	12th Dec. 8 a.m.	Coys sent down to ERQUINGHEM (6th Div. baths) at 2 hour interval.	
"	12 noon	6 officers and 150 men inoculated.	
"	13th 10 a.m.	Church service held by Rev. F STEWART C.F.	
	11.15 a.m	Orders received from 19th Bde ordering increased activity on part of Brigade to join enemy down to his ground.	
	14th 10 a.m. to 12 noon	Coy parades.	
	6 p.m.	Bale of presents received from H.M. Queen ALEXANDRA	
	9 p.m.	Enemy commenced shelling from of ARMENTIERES.	93 "
	11.30 p.m.	Some shells commenced landing in ASYLUM grounds. Coys ordered to dress and fall in in doors on ground floor.	
	15th 2 a.m.	Lull in hostile artillery fire for half an hour and coys dismissed, but kept in lower rooms.	
	2.30 a.m.	Renewal of hostile artillery fire. Shelling was directed indiscriminately against all parts of town and continued till 9 a.m. entire with a large number falling in the ASYLUM. About half the shells failed to burst. Although over 700 shells were fired over the ASYLUM and many into it, there were no casualties.	

5

Army Form C. 2118.

WAR DIARY
or
INTELLIGENCE SUMMARY.
(Erase heading not required.)

Instructions regarding War Diaries and Intelligence Summaries are contained in F.S. Regs., Part II. and the Staff Manual respectively. Title pages will be prepared in manuscript.

Hour, Date, Place		Summary of Events and Information	Remarks and references to Appendices
LUNATIC ASYLUM ARMENTIERES	15th 10 a.m.	Coy Parades.	
"	16th "	"	[A]
"	17th "	"	[A]
"	18th 10.30 a.m.	Draft of olivin (includes 12 for machine gun) arrived at 5.30 p.m. Inspection of battalion by Brigade Commander Brig-Genl. Hon. F. GORDON who expressed his satisfaction with appearance of battalion.	[A]
"	19th 8 a.m.	Orders received for battalion to take over trenches at HOUPLINES next night from MIDDLESEX Regt.	[A]
"	20th 10 a.m.	Church service conducted by Revd F STEWART C.F.	[A]
"	10.10 a.m.	Enemy commenced shelling ASYLUM with shrapnel and left explosive. 3 men wounded. Altogether about 20 shells were fired at ASYLUM, one entering Cook house and wounding men thus, one entered B Coys barrack room, full at the time, but only wounded one man slightly.	93rd
"	4.15 p.m.	Marched off to HOUPLINES.	
HOUPLINES	5 p.m.	Commenced taking over trenches.	
" (Trenches)	7.35 p.m.	Relief completed.	[A]
" (Trenches)	21st 8 a.m.	Orders received for increased activity. Active sniping to be practised and Safeheads pushed on:	[A]

(9.29.6) W 2794 100,000 5/14 H W V Forms/C. 2118/11

WAR DIARY
or
INTELLIGENCE SUMMARY.
(Erase heading not required.)

Army Form C. 2118.

Hour, Date, Place	Summary of Events and Information	Remarks and references to Appendices
POPERINGHE 22nd Dec 6.30pm (Tuesday)	Quiet Day. Lieut BOYD with patrol went through firing obtained wire and discovered Germans putting up new entanglement.	
9 a.m.	Captains of Bn H.Q's were inspected Interprises Bersan Lenten.	[5]
23rd Dec	Pipes were installed by 6th Divisional order.	
	9 a.m. had moving transport from West to East.	[6]
10½ p.m.	Lieut BARRIER arrived at 3½ a.m.	
24th Dec	Work carried out on communication trenches. A review made from C Coy G.a.a. B9. Gen. CONGREVE 18 Inf. Bd. (B2) visited in afternoon 15th Rgt.	[5]
25th Dec	Very quiet day. Germans came out of their trenches unarmed in afternoon and were seen to belong to 133rd and 134th Regiment.	
	The parties was remonstrated by Lieut ANDERSON. The Germans made it for leave to bury the dead. This was granted.	[6]
26th Dec 11 a.m.	A few shells were fired at and in rear of our front line going through the houses used as an orderly room.	
5 p.m.	Battalion relieved by Sherwood Foresters, Hy. My.14th Brigade going into Divisional Reserve at ARMENTIÈRES.	[5]

Army Form C. 2118.

WAR DIARY
or
INTELLIGENCE SUMMARY.
(Erase heading not required.)

Instructions regarding War Diaries and Intelligence Summaries are contained in F. S. Regs., Part II. and the Staff Manual respectively. Title pages will be prepared in manuscript.

Hour, Date, Place		Summary of Events and Information	Remarks and references to Appendices
HOUPLINES	26th	Relief carried out by platoons, one per company at quarter hour intervals.	
"	" 7.30 p.m	Relief completed	
"	" 8.35 "	1st Battalion all in billets.	
ARMENTIERES	27th		
	28th	Companies exercised in route marching	[?]
	26th	Companies received route marching. Information received from	[?]
		SOMERSET Lt Inf. that Capt W A HENDERSON's body had been found and buried by them.	[?]
	29th	Companies exercised in route marching	
	30th	Two Officers, Lieut BYRD and Lieut MOIR attended class of instruction in throwing hand grenades. Rest of battalion route marching	[?]
	31st	Class for throwing hand grenades increased by four men per company. Concert for men in Gymnasium at 5.30 p.m.	[?]

2/4/15

Jeward Thorpe
Captain and Adjutant

Appendix A1

Copy No. 9.

SPECIAL 8TH DIVISION OPERATION ORDER No......

CROIX DU BAC
1st December, 1914.

1. His Majesty The King will visit the 8th Division to-morrow arriving at CROIX DU BAC about 2.30.pm. The visit will occupy about one hour.

2. Troops will be formed up as shewn on the attached rough sketch All to be in position by 2.15.pm.

In addition to the units specified, the following will also be present with their respective formations:-

From each battalion in the trenches - One officer & 8 other ranks
From each Battery and Amm.Column - A quota to be detailed by C.R.A.
From every other unit   - A quota to be detailed.

3. Troops from the South of the River LYS will use the following bridges to get to their places:-

16th Infantry Brigade - BAC ST MAUR Bridge and trestle bridge ¾ mile below.

17th Infantry Brigade -⎫
18th Infantry Brigade -⎭ ERQUINGHEM Bridge.

19th Infantry Brigade - PONT DE NIEPPE.
to
Other troops any bridge, and/give way to infantry.

4. Troops will be drawn up in double rank on the left of the road. All officers will be formed up on the right of the road as shewn. Dress - Marching Order.

5. The route of the Royal Car is shewn in Green. It will be preceded at a distance of a 100 yards by a motor cyclist with a flag.

Troops will present arms by order of their N.C.Os. when the cyclist appears, and remain at the Present until the car is past.

6. Units will return independently to their billets as soon as the Royal Car has gone and the roads are clear.

7. Divisional Mounted Troops will block the side roads under orders already issued.

W.T.FURZE Colonel,

General Staff, 8th Division.

Normal distribution through Signal Service at 5.15.pm.

19th Infantry Brigade.

Your G.86. dated 9/12/14.

I beg to report that the enemy opened fire on my trenches at about 7.35.p.m. with Machine Guns AAA

Small parties of the enemy were seen advancing and fire from our trenches became general AAA In front of A.Coy & 5th S.R. the enemy got as far as the line of Willows in front of their trench. In front of B.Coy. a party got on to the ridge but quickly withdrew AAA We have not been able to see whether we inflicted any casualties on the enemy AAA The enemy's strength is judged to be at least equal to our own judging by the rifle fire AAA No hostile machine gun was definitely located but it is fairly certain that there is one in an emplacement about 100 yards S. of the big farm AAA Casualties at present ascertained are 3. 5th S.R. killed & 5 A. & S. Hrs. slightly wounded AAA A certain amount of wire has been damaged but can be easily repaired. AAA

One high explosive shell fell in trench occupied by 5th S.R. causing 2 deaths AAA.

Our shrapnel was bursting beautifully to meet an attack. It completely swept the ground in front of our trenches.

10.12.14.
8.25.p.m.

(Sd) H.B. Kirk Major,
Commg. A. & S. Hrs.

Certified true copy.

J. Thay, Captain,
Adjutant, A. & S. Hrs.

INTELLIGENCE SUMMARY
(Erase heading not required.)

Instructions regarding War Diaries and Intelligence Summaries are contained in F.S. Regs., Part II. and the Staff Manual respectively. Title pages will be prepared in manuscript.

Hour, Date, Place			Summary of Events and Information	Remarks and references to Appendices
ARMENTIERES	1st Jan?		New Years day spent in billets. Telegrams exchanged with first battalion and others. Men given new year's dinner from gifts sent out by various friends of the regiment.	93rd
"	"	5 p.m.	Orders received about relief next day, battalion to relieve Kings SHROPSHIRE Lt INFANTRY	
"	2nd Jan?.	10 a.m.	Reserve platoon (King's) marched off to take over L. Wets under Capt HEYS THOMSON	☒
"	"	2 p.m.	Transport moved off to new quarters in RUE DES ACQUETS under Lt BOYD.	
"	"	7 p.m.	Battalion marches off to BOIS GRENIER to take over trenches of KING'S SHROPSHIRE L.I.	
BOIS GRENIER	"	8 p.m.	Relief started. Way to trenches very muddy and deep. Trenches very wet and great difficulty found in carrying anything to trenches over nearly a mile of	
"	(Trenches) 3rd Jan?.	12.30 a.m.	Sudden ground. Relief completed: One man K.S.L.I. killed during relief, no other casualties. A good deal of firing at our stretcher bearers burying him. Communication in the trench impossible owing to Communication between A and C Companies.	
"	3rd Jan?		Two foot of water and deep mud. Companies worked all day trying to make trenches habitable, but water continued to gain. New trench & dugouts made by No 16 platoon. Telephone line laid to CULVERT FARM. Rations arrived & were late at rendezvous, CULVERT FARM and were very late up to trenches. Still very wet, heavy rain. Sniping by enemy active.	☒
"	4th Jan?	5 p.m.	Lieut HUTCHISON evacuated his support trench and went into CULVERT FARM, digging new trenches close by for his two platoons B.6.3. One man wounded in support trench (headquarters trench).	
"	"	3 p.m.	General GORDON went round our trenches and completed his round without boots, having had these sucked off by the mud. This kept on occurring to many of the men.	☒
"	5th Jan?		Still heavy rain and water rising in all trenches.	

INTELLIGENCE SUMMARY

(Erase heading not required.)

Instructions regarding War Diaries and Intelligence Summaries are contained in F. S. Regs., Part II. and the Staff Manual respectively. Title pages will be prepared in manuscript.

93rd

Hour, Date, Place		Summary of Events and Information	Remarks and references to Appendices
BOIS GRENIER Trenches	5th 11 a.m.	Our artillery shelled hostile trenches opposite and appeared to make very accurate shooting.	
" "	" 2 p.m.	Enemy started shelling BOIS GRENIER and then turned on our trenches. Some shells landed on the parapets of A Co's and close by but no casualties. Rain continued to make parapets and dug outs fall in.	[5]
" "	6th	Water still rising, having gained about a foot since the battalion came in on the 2nd. That Trenches only held by damming up communication trenches and baling. Headquarters turned about one foot in water except just near C. O's and telephone shelters. Communication on raised planks. No communication with Coys except by telephone and by night [?] across country. Trenches become quite untenable except in isolated patches. It was therefore settled to come out at night and start work behind.	[5]
	5 p.m.	Work begun on back parapet, a shallow trench about one foot deep being dug behind the back parapet and this parapet flattened and made bulletproof. Dam holding water out of headquarters support trench burst, and all men had to be moved out. Owing to difficulty in laying new telephone lines suddenly and as the C.O.'s and the telephone shelters still stood it was settled not to move headquarters as yet.	
	7th	There were practically no places left for the men to lie down and work on establishing a new firing line was continued all night. Some firing recommenced, especially on planks were still possible and steps were cut into the fire trenches, access to the recesses being across planks.	[5]

Forms/C. 2118/11.

INTELLIGENCE SUMMARY

(Erase heading not required.)

Instructions regarding War Diaries and Intelligence Summaries are contained in F.S. Regs, Part II, and the Staff Manual respectively. Title pages will be prepared in manuscript.

Hour, Date, Place	Summary of Events and Information	Remarks and references to Appendices
BOIS GRENIER 8th Jan. Tuesday	Men spent the day either in the wet trenches or in the new trench. This only gave 3 feet of cover. (Communication being impossible, men constantly exposed themselves but as the enemy was evidently as badly off only two casualties (one killed one wounded) were suffered. Orders received from 19th B.de to commence work on new breastwork, with shelters in front parapet. Headquarters moved into GRANDE FLAMENDRIE FARM. Major H.B. KIRK left battalion for hospital. Capt HYSLOP assumed command.	931st
6 P.M.	Draft of 70 men from H. Batt.n arrived.	
" " 9th Jan.s	Men still exposed if they moved about. One man killed. Work was ordered so as to complete 50 yards of breastwork with shelters. The material that arrived was found to be quite unsuitable, but about 30 yards was put up but not completed. The shelters were put up by R.E. and fatigue parties did the digging. Work continued from 10 p.m to 9 a.m. The difficulty experienced in collecting the various parts for a length of parapet with shelters was very great owing to the very bad road. The material had to be carried over. The way lay through fields knee deep in water and across some ditches 2 to 3 feet deep. Weather still wet, men getting very tired.	

Forms/C. 2118/11.

INTELLIGENCE SUMMARY

(Erase heading not required.)

Hour, Date, Place	Summary of Events and Information	Remarks and references to Appendices
BOIS GRENIER Dec-ber 10th	Arrangements made to again try and put up 50 yards of breastwork at night. Men had to set very still all day as communication was impossible and shelter very inadequate.	
" " 6 p.m.	A very wet night. R.E. material commenced arriving at 9 p.m. but was not all up till 2 a.m. What did arrive was totally inadequate and various essential parts were omitted. One of the shelters put up the night before fell in, damaging four men, fortunately not severely. At 2 a.m. it was decided to discontinue work as what was being done was perfectly useless. It was therefore settled that work for the night of the 11th should consist in putting up breastworks without shelters to be put up later. 3 reliefs of 40 men were ordered from the reserve company, and working parties	
11th Dec-ber 2 a.m.		
6 p.m. to 12th – 3 a.m.	were ordered from the firing line platoons. Ration issue and billets for Reserve Platoons transferred to NEW FARM making carriage of rations & issue much easier. Work was carried on all this time and made good progress.	
9 a.m. 11 a.m.	Or.C. Coys' breastwork. Some old graves were met with, delaying and in A Coys some old latrines impeded the work. 1 officer per coy and 3 N.C.Os per coy met at Bde Hd Qrs and were taken to R.E. works at ERQUINGHEM to see sample breastwork. The conclusion come to was that the type was totally unsuitable and not nearly strong enough.	

Hour, Date, Place		Summary of Events and Information	Remarks and references to Appendices
BOIS GRENIER trenches	12th 6p.m.	Work continued on breastworks as the night before; revetting them with brushwood hurdles, and putting traverses between the various lengths of breastwork.	[S]
"	13th 3a.m.	Ceased work for night.	
"	" 11.a.m	Enemy put 2 shells against new breastwork erected by D Coy, the first shell killing 7 men and wounding 2 others.	
"	" 5.45h	Relief by 1st Cameronians began.	[S]
"	" 8.45h	Relief completed.	[S] 93rd
GRIS POT	14th	All in billets in RUE DELETTREE near GRIS POT	[S]
"	"	A rest day. Reserve company (B Coy) sent to baths at BAC ST MAUR	
"	15th	Rested. 100 men went to baths at BAC ST MAUR. Capt R.T.NICOL (4th Batt'n) joined and took over C Coy.	[S]
"	16th	Lt. Col. R.C. GORE arrived and took over Command.	
"	17th 11.a.m	Church service held by Rev. F Stewart - C.F.	
"	" 12 noon	Practiced grenade squads (one per company). Brigadier decided to adopt system of 5 day reliefs, A & S H'ds relieving MIDDLESEX and holding trenches for 5 days at a time.	[S]

INTELLIGENCE SUMMARY

(Erase heading not required.)

Hour, Date, Place			Summary of Events and Information	Remarks and references to Appendices
GRIS POT	18th	10.30 a.m.	Conference at Bn. Hd. Qrs. between O.C. 2nd A.&S.H. and 1st MIDDLESEX re taking over trenches.	
"	"	4.30 p.m.	Battalion marched off to LA VESEE to take over trenches from MIDDLESEX regiment. Relief started at 5.30 p.m.	
LA VESEE (trenches)	"	9 p.m.	Relief completed. No firing. Three platoons could not be accommodated. Firing line B Co's 3 platoons D Co's 3 platoon. Two platoons A Co's in support. Trenches taken over were in bad state, fire trenches impossible and only tenable in places. Very little work had been done with breastworks. One left (D Co's) was opposite Saxons who never fired, so work proceeded by day. Room was made to accommodate 1 platoon in support.	S.
"	19th			
"	"	5.30 p.m.	A Coy's 2 platoons in support were withdrawn for day, returning to trenches at dark. These support trenches were very wet. Work carried on breastworks, and continued throughout night. (Command trench for platoon in support behind centre (C Co's).	S.
"	20th	12.30 p.m.	A few rounds fired by our artillery at hostile trenches.	
"	"	3 p.m.	Enemy fired two rounds at BURNT FARM. No damage.	
"	"	6.30 p.m.	Work continued on breastworks and C Coy's support trench. 2nd Lieut J.P.YOUNGER joined.	S.

INTELLIGENCE SUMMARY

(Erase heading not required.)

Hour, Date, Place	Summary of Events and Information	Remarks and references to Appendices
LA VESÉE trenches 21st 5.30 p.m.	General Gordon (comdg 19th Infy Bde) visited trenches.	☒
" " " 22nd 6.30 p.m.	Two platoons MIDDLESEX came to assist in erecting breastworks.	
" " " 23rd 5 p.m.	Work continued in erecting breastworks, assisted by platoons MIDDLESEX.	☒
" " " 8 p.m.	Relief by MIDDLESEX Regt commenced.	
L'ARMÉE 24th 11 a.m.	Relief completed. Went into billets. Battalion divisional Reserve. Church service held by Rev. F. Stewart C.F.	☒
" 25th	Route marching by companies. Lieut LIDDELL sent away sick.	2nd ☒
" 5 p.m.	Draft of 95 men under 2nd Lieut I.M. MILLER arrived	
" 26th	Route marching by companies.	
" 9 p.m.	Orders received to be prepared to move at 5 minutes notice commencing 9 a.m. 27th.	☒
" 27th 9 a.m.	Kaiser's birthday. News having been received of large concentration of enemy about LILLE, an attack was expected. The battalion stood to arms, but as all was quiet dismissed at 9 a.m. Warned to be ready to turn out at short notice.	☒
" 28th	Battalion took over trenches at LA VESÉE from MIDDLESEX Regt. B, A, D coys in front line, C Co in support.	☒

INTELLIGENCE SUMMARY

(Erase heading not required.)

93rd

Hour, Date, Place	Summary of Events and Information	Remarks and references to Appendices
LA VESÉE (Rue du) 2g E 11 a.m.	Heavy rifle fire by Germans against one of our aeroplanes. No damage. Work on breastworks continued. Defence of supporting points arranged.	—
" " 30 E	Took over additional section of line from 5th Scottish Rifles. Work continued on breastworks and supporting points.	—
" " 31st	Work continued on breastworks and supporting points, connecting these by fire trench. Work carried out on wire entanglements, strengthening those	—
5/2/15.		

James Hope
Capt & Adjutant
2nd Argyll & Sutd Highrs.

19th Inf.Bde.
6th Div.

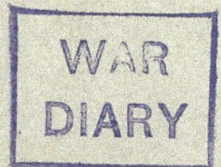

2nd BATTN. THE ARGYLL & SUTHERLAND HIGHLANDERS.

F E B R U A R Y

1 9 1 5

INTELLIGENCE SUMMARY
(Erase heading not required.)

Instructions regarding War Diaries and Summaries are contained in F. S. Regs., Part II. and the Staff Manual respectively. Title pages will be prepared in manuscript.

Hour, Date, Place		Summary of Events and Information	Remarks and references to Appendices
Nr BOIS GRENIER	1st February	A very wet day. Brig General Gordon came round the Trenches in the evening.	AA
	2nd " 12.30pm	R.F.A reported hostile Trenches in front of our left	AA
	2.30pm	Part of "A" Company's trench shelled. They find who not occupied, thus loss was	
L'ARMÉE	" 6pm	Company relieved by 1st Bn. Middlesex Regt and went into billets at L'ARMÉE	AA
	" 8pm	Relief complete. Bn in Divisional Reserve.	
	3rd " 10am	Coy Parade. 200 men to bathe at BAC ST MAUR	AA
	" 7pm	Working party of 3 Platoons went to help Middlesex Regt	
	4th " 10am	Coy Parade. 200 men to bath at BAC ST MAUR	
	" 2pm	130 men warned for Entire.	
	" 7pm	Working party of 3 Platoons went to help Middlesex Regt	
	" 7.15pm	Heavy Artillery firing began in the direction of RUE du BOIS, then seem	
	"	of Flares etc. Musketry + Machine gun fire	
	" 7.25pm	Received orders stand by	
	" 7.40pm	Running order to Entre on + Counterattack on L'ARMÉE, then sudden	
	" 5pm	Received orders to Entrain to Billets but C & D coys to line up and attack	
	"	Firing gradually stopped. The Germans had evidently made inroads on attack	
	"	for in some places a few men near left the trenches, taking arms and left them	
	"	soon to return. Or would there have been very few casualties from these guns	
	"	fire.	
	5th " 10.15am	Brig gen Keir commanding VI Division inspected the Bn	AA
	6th " 10 am	Company Parade.	AA
	" 4.30pm	Enemy shelled ARMENTIÈRES with incendiary shells. Half a platoon of H.Q	AA
Nr BOIS GRENIER	7th " 10am	Company Parade. Relieved John Middlesex Regt on the Trenches Rebuy	AA
	" 5.15pm	Relief off & relieve 7.45pm	
	8th "	completed 7.45pm	
	"	Work on trenches continued. Sniping very heavy on the left + front	AA
	"	Captain J C Scott arrived and took over command of A Coy	

INTELLIGENCE SUMMARY

(Erase heading not required.)

Summaries are contained in F.S. Regs., Part II, and the Staff Manual respectively. Title pages will be prepared in manuscript.

9377

Hour, Date, Place		Summary of Events and Information	Remarks and references to Appendices
Nr BOIS GRENIER	9th February 2 pm	Two men wounded by snipers in EFF.Y on our Extreme left. [Brig General GORDON visited our trenches after dark]	NA
	10th "	One man wounded. Look continued during the night. Capt THORPE left to take up Staff appointment and Major H.G. Hyslop 2nd in temporarily the duties of Adjutant	NA
	11th "	2 men killed by snipers on the left of our line. [These men were buried by the Rev. STEWART Chaplain near RATION FARM]	NA
	"	8 pm Captain R. Nicol (4 Terr) attached to our wounded in the side (knee). Work continued during the night	NA
	12th " "	Two men wounded in trenches. Relieved by 1/4th Middlesex Regt. (1 casualty.) Returned to billets.	NA
	" 6.15 pm	RHE L'ARMEE Relief completed 8.15 pm	NA
L'ARMEE	13th " 8.15 pm	Several shells fell near South End of billets.	NA
	" 3 pm	100 men to BAC St MAUR Baths	NA
	14th " 10.30 am	Parade Service	NA
	15th " 8.30 am	Stoop & bayonets. Dismissed 7.15 am	NA
	" 10 am	Company Parade. (12th Reinforcement)	NA
	16th " 1 pm	Draft of 33 men arrived	NA
	" 6.45 am	Stood to arms	NA
	" 9.30 am	C.Os Parade and inspection of clothing & equipment A + B Coys	NA
	17th " 9.30 am	C.Os inspection of clothing + equipment C + D Coys	NA
Nr BOIS GRENIER	" 5.10 pm	Marched off to relieve Middlesex Regt in the Trenches near BOIS GRENIER. Relief completed without casualty 8 pm	NA
	18th "	Sniping began very early in the morning & was very persistent till about 9 am Several Light and Flare had been used by the Germans very freely	NA

Casualties during the night
1 off 2 L/Company killed 2nd NCOs 1 man & 1 Telegram

Form C.2118/11.
1247 W 3299 200,000 (E) 8/14 J.B.C. & A.

Hour, Date, Place	Summary of Events and Information	Remarks and references to Appendices
BOIS GRENIER 19th February 5:30am	Support Trenches shelled. 20 casualties. Enemy sniping very persistent.	
" " 2:30–4:37pm	Artillery on both sides shelled trenches. One man killed by sniper.	
" " 7pm	2 Platoons Canadian Infantry came down the attached. They were billeted up in the Trenches with "A" & "D" Coys.	M
	The following names appeared in the Gazette dated 17/2/15 as mentioned in Despatches. Major Kirk, Major Hyslop, Capt Thorpe, Lieut Clark, Lieut Liddell, Sgt Maj Kerr, Pt J Campbell, Pt J Haddon	93rd
20th February 8am	One man killed one wounded in D Coy by snipers	M
" 7pm	Two Platoons 4th Canadians relieved platoons in the trenches.	
	Major HB Kirk left for home 1pm.	
21st " 10:30am	Service in BILLET FARM for those free.	
" " 2pm	One man killed by sniper & one wounded	M
" " 3pm	Enemy shelled C Coy Trenches.	
	The following Honours have been given in the London Gazette of 18th February to be Brevet Lt Col. Major Hyslop DSO. Capt Thorpe DSO. Major Kirk to be Brevet Lt Col. Major Hyslop DSO. Capt Thorpe DSO. Lieuts Clark, Liddell (3rd Bn) and Sergt Major Kerr, Military Cross.	
" " 3:30pm	"C" Coy Trenches shelled.	
" " 7pm	Canadians left the Trenches. Relief completed 8:30pm. No casualties	M
22nd "	Heavy Fog. One Sergeant of A Coy killed. Relieved by 1/Middlesex Regt.	M
L'ARMEE 6:30pm		
23rd " 10am	200 men Bath. BAC St MAUR	M
" 2pm	200 men Bath.	
24th " 10am	Company Parades. 200 Bath.	M
" 7:30pm	Digging party from C Coy at Second Line	M

Hour, Date, Place		Summary of Events and Information	Remarks and references to Appendices
L'ARMÉE 25th February	10am	Company parades. 200 men to Baths.	
	7.30pm	Company working party of A Coy on 2nd line	
26th "	10am	Company parade.	
	6pm	Reinforcement of 3 Officers, Captain Narellan-Ramsay Lieuts Macpherson	
	"	+ Gillespie + 30 other ranks.	
	7.30	Working party of B Coy on 2nd line.	
27th "	10am	Company Parade.	
	6.10pm	Marched off to relieve 1/Middlesex Regt in the Trenches. Relief completed	93rd
Nr BOIS GRENIER	8.20pm		
28th "		Work on trenches continued during the night.	

H.J. Huyshe Major
O/c 1 coy 1 A+S Highlanders

19th Inf.Bde.
6th Div.

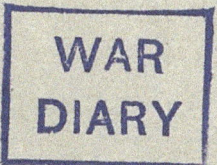

2nd BATTN. THE ARGYLL & SUTHERLAND HIGHLANDERS.

M A R C H

1 9 1 5

INTELLIGENCE SUMMARY

(Erase heading not required.)

Instructions regarding War Diaries and Intelligence Summaries are contained in F.S. Regs., Part II. and the Staff Manual respectively. Title pages will be prepared in manuscript.

Hour, Date, Place	Summary of Events and Information	Remarks and references to Appendices
Nr BOIS GRENIER 1st March 8am	Heavy shelling of gun positions behind our lines. One shell through our Aid Post	/tt
2nd " 2 pm		9³
" 10am–12pm	Enemy gun positions again shelled	/tt
" 11am	One order killed in fire trench by sniper	
" 7.15pm	Major Gordon visited our trenches	
3rd " 11am	Trenches shelled on left of line no casualties	/tt
4th " 11am	Trenches shelled & part of breastwork destroyed. No casualties	/tt
" 6.30pm	Relieved by 1 Middlesex Regt. Relief completed 5.30 pm. One slight casualty	/tt
L'ARMÉE 5th "	Cleaning up.	/tt
6th " 11.15am	G.O.C 11th Div. inspected billets & men but parade was cancelled	/tt
"	Heavy rain	/tt
7th " 10.30	Private Service	/tt
8th " 9am	Company Parade	/tt
9th " 9am	Company Parade	/tt
" 6.15pm	Relieved 1 Middlesex Regt in the trenches. Relief completed 9 pm. One man killed & one wounded.	/tt
Nr BOIS GRENIER 10th " 4am	Heavy artillery fire on our left.	/tt
" 5.30am	Artillery fire opened for a few minutes by Canadian supporting batteries on our right & Heavy Guns from Armées S.W. of NEUVE CHAPELLE	Appendices A and B
	1st Army made successful attack on neighbourhood of NEUVE CHAPELLE	
	692 prisoners taken.	
" 11.30am	We opened rapid fire on enemy's trenches while artillery bombarded them. There was no reply. We caused no opposition and gathered trophy right	
" 11.50am	Bombardment ceased. Many dead lot were made in enemy's trenches but the Bois was empty returned in a feeble way and entire one shell hit the Lieutenant Ivry little damage. One man killed

1247 W 3299 200,000 (E) 8/14 J.B.C. & A. Forms/C. 2118/11.

INTELLIGENCE SUMMARY

(Erase heading not required.)

Summaries are contained in F. S. Regs., Part II. and the Staff Manual respectively. Title pages will be prepared in manuscript.

Hour, Date, Place	Summary of Events and Information	Remarks and references to Appendices
Nr BOIS GRENIER 11th March 9am	Commenced our heavy fire and our artillery bombarded German trenches. Enemy did not reply	Appendix C
" 3pm	Enemy fired 20 shells into CHAPELLE ARMENTIERES	
12th " 12.39am	17th Brigade on our left attacked village of L'EPINETTE and approx.	
" 4.30am	16th Brigade opened a heavy fire on German trenches for a few minutes	
"	10th Army attack near NEUVE CHAPELLE continues	
13th " 1.30pm	Some more men killed by snipers	
" 11pm	Heavy sniping and machine gun fire. Many Verey lights, which we returned	Appendix D
14th " 7pm	One man killed & Lieut Boyd wounded	
15th "	11 men of the 73rd are found at ALBERT VERHAEGHE's Farm near LA VESEE	Appendix E
"	Reinforced by us at RATION FARM. 2 men are found at a Farm 1/2 mile S.E. of the Farm and Recon by us to BURNT FARM	
" 6.45pm	Relieved in trenches by 2nd R. Welsh Fusiliers. Relay completed 9.30pm	
L'ARMEE 16th "	Went into Billets in L'ARMEE	
"	Captain J Kennedy took over the A/Adjutancy from Major H.G.Heyslop who had been acting Adjt. Capt Myrie - S/Lts Lock, Annie to Gris Pot	
17th " 6.15pm	Battalion changed billet from L'Armée to Croix Cornuin in trenches near Hameau- Farm - relief completed 10p.m. - Headqrs Coy & Battalion in trenches	
18th "	Shelled in trenches. 8pm Brigadier General Gordon inspected trenches	
19th " 4pm		
20th "	In trenches - 1 man wounded. 2nd Lieut Boyd returned but was again wounded on his way to Hosptl. Lieut 4 Munro & 5 N.C.O's. 2nd Lt Stafford (6th Btn) attached to us. In trenches for 24 hours	
21st "	In trenches - 3 men severely wounded. Col. Jelf - who places N. Stafford attached for his trenches	

Hour, Date, Place	Summary of Events and Information	Remarks and references to Appendices
22nd March 1915 In Trenches	1 man severely wounded	9/2
23rd " In Trenches	2 men killed - relieved by 1st Cameronian. Relief completed 9.30 p.m. Nr. Stafford attached slightly wounded during relief	9/2
24th " In billets	1 man near Pris Pot	
25th " In billet	"mule" marching fire control	
26th " In billet	"mule" marching - fire control. Lectures on sniper formation	9/2
27th " In billet		
28th " 10.30 a.m.	Church parade on hill - paraded to trenches 6.45 p.m. relieved 1st Cameronian - relief completed 9 p.m. 1 man severely wounded	9/2
29th " In Trenches	Shelled by enemy at 3.30 p.m. & 8.30 p.m. 1 man wounded 1 man died in field ambulance	9/2
30th " In Trenches	Trenches + Laphead's shelled 4 a.m. 1 man wounded	9/2
31st " In Trenches	1 man killed 5 wounded (serious) by snipers - 2nd Lt Welsh joined from 3rd Battalion	9/2

J Kennedy, Captain.
Adjt. 2nd Argyll & Suth Highrs.

19th Inf.Bde.
6th Div.

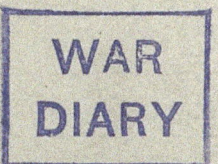

2nd BATTN. THE ARGYLL & SUTHERLAND HIGHLANDERS.

A P R I L

1 9 1 5

Instructions regarding War Diaries and Intelligence
Summaries are contained in F. S. Regs., Part II.
and the Staff Manual respectively. Title pages
will be prepared in manuscript.

INTELLIGENCE SUMMARY

(Erase heading not required.)

Hour, Date, Place			Summary of Events and Information	Remarks and references to Appendices
1.4.15.	Rue Bois Grenier	In Trenches.	1 Man killed and five wounded.	JM
2.4.15	—	"	In trenches. 1 Man wounded Seven 4 Officers M.C.O's Slightly Wounded.	JM
3.4.15	—	"	In trenches. Shelled and many grenades fired. Heavy shelling early morning and all day to the north.	JM
4.4.15	—	"	In trenches. All day. Moved to Billets evening. No casualties during operation of Relief.	JM
5.4.15	Erquinghem	In Billets.	Day occupied by men cleaning up. Parties to Baths at Erquinghem and Bac St Maur.	JM
6.4.15	—	"	In Billets. Practicing bomb throwing. Route Marching and drill. Parties to Baths.	JM
7.4.15	—	"	In Billets. — Do —	JM
8.4.15	—	"	In Billets all day. Practicing Bomb throwing. Route marching & billets.	JM
8 p.m.	Rue de Bois	Took over trenches near Rue de Bois. Splendid trenches. Garden in front of C. O's dug out in Reserve trench.		JM
9.4.15	—	"	In trenches. 1 man wounded.	JM
10.4.15	—	"	In trenches. General Gordon inspected trenches - Evening enemy signalling with Search light.	JM

Instructions regarding War Diaries and Intelligence Summaries are contained in F.S. Regs., Part II. and the Staff Manual respectively. Title pages will be prepared in manuscript.

INTELLIGENCE SUMMARY

(Erase heading not required.)

Hour, Date, Place			Summary of Events and Information	Remarks and references to Appendices
11.4.15	Rue du Bois	In trenches	1 Man killed. Reports asked for on paper Wadis - trench covers for rifle - number of mouth organs wanted for men - if blanket coat uniform preferred to blankets - wire breakers attached to bayonet - Dirty dixies.	JK
12.4.15	"	In trenches	1 man wounded. Hostile aeroplane hit. Report on Field Kitchens. 2nd Lieut Mori from London Scottish and Lieut Macnab from Glasgow Highlanders joined. Left trenches in evening for Billets.	JK
13.4.15	Gns Pot.	In Billets	Cleaning up.	JK
14.4.15	"	In Billets	Practice Alarm - Battalion turned out complete in 25 minutes - Draft strength 25 joined.	JK
15.4.15	"	In Billets	Lieutenant Hutchison left for England. Inspection of Grenadiers.	JK
16.4.15	"	In Billets	Reports on Sanitary conditions for Summer. Practice Charging with bayonet. Parade under Grenadier Officer.	JK

X

INTELLIGENCE SUMMARY

(Erase heading not required.)

Hour, Date, Place	Summary of Events and Information	Remarks and references to Appendices
17.4.15. Gris Pots. In Billets.	Practised Charging with bayonet - bomb throwing - musketry.	JY
18.4.15. " "	In Billets all day. - D° - D° - D° - Draft of 25 joined.	JY
9p.m. - " Rue du Bois	In trenches took over trenches near Rue du Bois. No Casualties	JY
19.4.15 "	In Trenches. - 1 man wounded.	JY
20.4.15 "	In Trenches. - 2nd Lieut. Satterfield London Scottish joined. Much big Gun fire heard up North (Battle for Hill 60).	JY
21.4.15 "	In Trenches -	JY
22.4.15 "	In Trenches - 1st Telescopic sight arrived.	JY
23.4.15 "	In Trenches - Relieved to Billets Gris Pot. Relief complete 10p.m.	JY
24.4.15 Gris Pot. In Billets	Cleaning up. 200 men. "A" & "D" Coys. to Baths at Vac St Maur	JY
25.4.15 " " In Billets	Church Service for all denominations. (Voluntary) Large attendance.	JY

INTELLIGENCE SUMMARY

(Erase heading not required.)

Summaries are contained in F. S. Regs., Part II. and the Staff Manual respectively. Title pages will be prepared in manuscript.

Hour, Date, Place		Summary of Events and Information	Remarks and references to Appendices
26. 4. 15	Griffot	In Billets. Drill, Musketry, Bayonet fighting, Bomb throwing, 200 men "C" & "B" Coy. Baths at Bac St Maur. Brig. Genl. & Gordon Comm. 19th I. Bde. inspected Mervin Billets.	JK
27. 4. 15	"	In Billets. Drill etc. same as 26.4.15. Party at Baths 2nd Heavy gun fire heard up North. (Battle for Calais) Draft of 50 men joined from Base (60% composed of wounded & sick men returning)	JK
28. 4. 15	"	In Billets all day; 200 men at Baths. Drill 10 ex cutting tool.	JK
—	Rude Boo	In trenches Took over trenches, no casualties.	JK
29. 4. 15	"	In trenches. 1 Cpl. killed, 1 man wounded.	JK
30. 4. 15	"	In trenches, 1 man killed.	JK

JK Thomas Capt. and
J. Thomson Capt.

19th Inf.Bde.
6th Div.

Battn. with Bde.
joined 27th Div.
31.5.15.

WAR DIARY

2nd BATTN. THE ARGYLL & SUTHERLAND HIGHLANDERS.

M A Y

1 9 1 5

WAR DIARY or INTELLIGENCE SUMMARY.

(Erase heading not required.)

Hour, Date, Place	Summary of Events and Information	Remarks and references to Appendices
1st May, 1915, Rue du Bois	In Trenches. Fuel for heating purposes discontinued the round.	JK
2nd May 1915, "	In Trenches. Respirators issued to Battalion (Anti Gas)	JK
3rd May 1915, "	In Trenches during day, left trenches at night and proceeded to Billets. Relief carried out without any casualties.	JK / JK
4th May 1915, Gris Pot	In Billets. Day spent in cleaning up.	JK
5th May 1915, "	In Billets. Drill etc – keeping fit.	JK
6th May 1915, "	In Billets. Drill etc – keeping fit.	JK
7th May 1915, "	In Billets. Battalion held in readiness to move at a moments notice. Did not move.	JK
8th May 1915, "	In Billets all day. Took over trenches at night – no casualties	JK
9th May 1915, Rue du Bois	In Trenches. Respirators inspection & practising quick adjustment.	JK

Instructions regarding War Diaries and Intelligence Summaries are contained in F.S. Regs, Part II. and the Staff Manual respectively. Title pages will be prepared in manuscript.

WAR DIARY or INTELLIGENCE SUMMARY.

(Erase heading not required.)

Hour, Date, Place	Summary of Events and Information	Remarks and references to Appendices
10th May 1915, Rue du Bois	In Trenches. 1 man severely wounded.	JK
11th May 1915, "	In Trenches. Usual Trench Routine.	JK
12th May 1915, "	In Trenches. — do —	JK
13th May 1915, "	In Trenches all day. Removed from Trenches to Billets at night. No Casualties	JK
14th May 1915, Brie Rect	In Billets. 25% of Blankets withdrawn from the Battalion.	JK
15th May 1915, "	In Billets. Practised A.Coy. in attacking trench, changing tarafet, Bomb throwing wire cutting.	JK
16th May 1915, "	In Billets. Church Services Church of Scotland, Church of England and Roman Catholic.	JK

WAR DIARY
or
INTELLIGENCE SUMMARY.
(Erase heading not required.)

Instructions regarding War Diaries and Intelligence Summaries are contained in F. S. Regs., Part II. and the Staff Manual respectively. Title pages will be prepared in manuscript.

Hour, Date, Place	Summary of Events and Information	Remarks and references to Appendices
17th May 1915, Gnu Pot	In Billets. Drill etc. Keeping fit.	JK
18th May 1915, "	In Billets — do —	JK
19th May, Rue du Bois	In Billets during the day. Took over trenches in Rue du Bois at night. No casualties.	JK
20th May 1915, "	In trenches, two platoons to 1st Battalion A.S.H. for instruction. Many old 93rd & 98th comrades found among the Officers and men.	JK
21st May 1915, "	In trenches, 2 men wounded. Another 2 platoons of 10th A.S.H. replaced above mentioned platoons and stayed for about 12 hours.	JK JK
22nd May, 1915, "	In trenches, 1 man wounded. Gas alarm.	
23rd May 1915, "	In trenches, 1 man wounded. Church Service for men in Billets. Found Battn. moved to Billets at Gnu Pot at night. No casualties during relief.	JK

INTELLIGENCE SUMMARY.
(Erase heading not required.)

Hour, Date, Place	Summary of Events and Information	Remarks and references to Appendices
24th May, 1915, Envo Pot. In Billets	"Stand to" at 1.30 a.m. on account of attack on right by 2nd K. Div.	JK
25th May, 1915, In Billets	Confined to Billets waiting orders to move at short notice in support of line.	JK
26 May, 1915, In Billets	"C" Coy practise attack on trenches. Concert held in Billets in the evening. B. Genl. Godord Hands.	JK
27 May, 1915, In Billets	"D" Coy practise attack on trenches. 2nd Lieut R. Rogie joins.	JK
28 May 1915, In Billets	During the day, took over trenches Rue du Bois at night. No Casualties during relief.	JK
" Rue du Bois, In Trenches	Lieut H.A. Campbell and reinforcements of 34 machine gunners joined from 3rd, C4, B?	JK JK
29th May, 1915, In Trenches	1 man killed & 1 man wounded.	JK
30th May, 1915, In Trenches	Same in which stray Medical Officer (Officer of Coy in Billets hut with enemies shells. One French woman & three children wounded.	JK

INTELLIGENCE SUMMARY.

(Erase heading not required.)

Instructions regarding War Diaries and Intelligence Summaries are contained in F.S. Regs., Part II. and the Staff Manual respectively. Title pages will be prepared in manuscript.

Hour, Date, Place	Summary of Events and Information	Remarks and references to Appendices
31st May, 1915, Rue du Bois	1st Battalion came into the trenches on our left, having arrived with 27th Division from Ypres. Old comrades met and exchanged greetings. This is the first time the two picket Battalions have met together for sometime. The Battalion looked quite fit and healthy after their trials at Ypres. 19th Infantry Brigade attached to 27th Division. The 6th Division proceeded to Ypres. We were sorry to have to leave that Division as we had made a good many friends amongst the Staff, Artillery & other Corps during our seven months on this winter good past.	J.W. Hassit Captain Adjt 1/Argyll & Suth'd H⁴rs J.H.

Forms/C. 2118/11

27TH DIVISION
19TH INFY BDE

2ND BN A. & S. HDRS
JUN-JLY 1915

19th Infantry Brigade.

27th Division.

(Battn. with Bde. left 6th Division on 31.5.15)

WAR DIARY

2nd BATTN. THE ARGYLL AND SUTHERLAND HIGHLANDERS.

J U N E

1 9 1 5

Attached:

Appendices A1, A2 & A3.

Original
19th Brigade

181/6015

War Diary

of

2nd Battalion Argyll & Sutherland Highlanders,

From 1st June, 1915 to 30th June, 1915,

Vol XI

– Index, –

Pages. 1 to 5 – Summary of Events
                  and Information.
Page. 6 & 7 – Appx. A 1.
Page. 8 – Appx. B 2.
Page. 9 & 10 – Appx. B 3.

Army Form C. 2118.

WAR DIARY
or
INTELLIGENCE SUMMARY.

(Erase heading not required.)

Instructions regarding War Diaries and Intelligence Summaries are contained in F.S. Regs., Part II. and the Staff Manual respectively. Title pages will be prepared in manuscript.

Hour, Date, Place		Summary of Events and Information	Remarks and references to Appendices
1st June, 1915	Rue du Bois. In Trenches	112th Battery Royal Field Artillery left from supporting 19th Bde, Greetings exchanged.	JK
2nd June, 1915	"	In Trenches during day, proceeded to Billets at Gris Pot at night. Relieved by R.W. Fusiliers	JK
3rd June, 1915	Gris Pot	In Billets. 200 men proceeded to Ypu River to Bathe.	JK
4th June, 1915	"	In Billets. 200 men proceeded to Ypu River by Ypres. Lecture delivered by Gas Expert. Took over trenches from Cameronians at night - no casualties.	JK
	Bois Grenier		
5th June, 1915	"	In Trenches. Our old Billets Farm shelled for first time. 1 man killed & 3 wounded R.W.F.	JK
6th June, 1915	"	In Trenches. Trenches & Battalion inspected by Major General T, D'O. Snow, C.B. Commanding 27th Division.	JK

Army Form C. 2118.

WAR DIARY
of
INTELLIGENCE SUMMARY
(Erase heading not required.)

Hour, Date, Place		Summary of Events and Information	Remarks and references to Appendices
7th June, 1915, Bois Grenier	In Trenches.	1 man killed.	JW
8 June 1915	In Trenches.	3 men wounded.	JW
9th June, 1915	In Trenches.		JW
10th June, 1915	In Trenches.	1 man wounded. Battalion proceeded to Billets at 'Erin Pot'. in the evening. Relieved by R.W. Fusiliers. No casualties during relief.	JW
11th June, 1915, Erin Pot	In Billets.	Cleaning up.	JW
12 June 1915	In Billets.	during day. Took over trenches at Rue du Bois. 2 men wounded.	JW
13th June 1915 Rue du Bois	In Trenches.	One man wounded. Trenches heavily shelled. German trenches shelled with mortars from our trenches.	JW
14 June 1915	In Trenches.	B.General Hon. F. Gordon C.B, D.S.O. vacated Command of 19th Infantry Brigade. Succeeded by Lieut. Col. J.R. Robertson, C.M.G. 1st Battalion Cameronians 'Highlanders'. Farewell message from Brig General Gordon received. See Appx. A1.	JW

Army Form C. 2118.

3

WAR DIARY
INTELLIGENCE SUMMARY

(Erase heading not required.)

Instructions regarding War Diaries and Intelligence Summaries are contained in F. S. Regs., Part II. and the Staff Manual respectively. Title pages will be prepared in manuscript.

Hour, Date, Place		Summary of Events and Information	Remarks and references to Appendices
15th June, 1915. Rue du Bois	In Trenches.		JW
16th June, 1915 — " —	In Trenches.	Lieut. J.A.A. Moir killed and 1 man killed.	JW
17th June, 1915 — " —	In Trenches.		JW
18th June, 1915 — " —	In Trenches.	C.S.M. Markey & 3 n.c.o.'s men wounded. Trenches heavily shelled in the morning. Relieved by R.W. Fusiliers at night and proceeded to billets at Rue Robt. (one man of above died of wounds, 10 cases.)	JW
19th June, 1915 Rue Rob.	In Billets.	Vicinity of Billets heavily shelled by enemy's heavy artillery.	JW
20th June, 1915 — " —	In Billets.	Billets shelled. 3 men wounded. Took over trenches at Burnt Farm in the evening, from 1st Cameronians. No Casualties.	JW
21st June, 1915 Mt. Rue du Bois	In Trenches.	1 N.C.O. wounded on patrol duty near the enemy's trenches. Died of wounds same day	JW

1247 W 3299 200,000 (E) 8/14 J.B.C. & A. Forms/C. 2118/11.

Army Form C. 2118.

WAR DIARY
or
INTELLIGENCE SUMMARY
(Erase heading not required.)

Hour, Date, Place	Summary of Events and Information	Remarks and references to Appendices
22nd June, 1915. Mr. Rue du Bois.	In Trenches. (night 21/22.6.15.) Strong Patrol of Battalion from "D" & "B" Companies reconnoitred enemy's trenches with a view to procuring information as to what troops occupied the trenches opposite in accordance with instructions received from Head Quarters. Came in contact with a large body of the enemy, killing several and procuring the information required. Casualties 1 man killed, 1 man wounded & missing & 1 man dangerously wounded & 1 man wounded. Severe. Evening 22.6.15. 1 man wounded.	Congratulations from Br. Genl. Comm'dg 19th Inf. Bde. received. See appx. A. 2. & A. 3. JW
23 June, 1915. Mr. Rue du Bois. In trenches.		JW
24 June 1915, Rue du Bois. In trenches.	Battalion moved from trenches Mr. Burnt Farm to trenches at Rue du Bois. No Casualties.	JW
25 June, 1915. In trenches	1 man killed.	JW

Army Form C. 2118.

WAR DIARY
or
INTELLIGENCE SUMMARY

(Erase heading not required.)

Instructions regarding War Diaries and Intelligence Summaries are contained in F. S. Regs., Part II. and the Staff Manual respectively. Title pages will be prepared in manuscript.

Hour, Date, Place	Summary of Events and Information	Remarks and references to Appendices
26th June 1915 Rue du Bois	In Trenches. 1 man wounded.	J.K.
27th June 1915 " "	In Trenches. 4 men wounded. Battalion rel'd by 1st Battn. A. & S. H'rs. and proceeded to Billets at Gris Pot.	J.K.
28 June 1915 Gris Pot, in Billets	In Billets. Parties to Bath. General cleaning up.	J.K.
29 June 1915 " "	In Billets. Large number of men inoculated against Typhoid. Parties to Bath.	J.K.
30 June 1915 " "	In Billets. do do Divine Service held for Church of Scotland & Roman Catholics	J.K.

J Kennedy Captain
Acting Adj't 3/Arg. Suth. Highr.

Forms/C. 2118/11.

A P P E N D I C E S

    A1.
    A2.
    A3.

Farewell message to 19th Infantry
Brigade (and attached troops)
Sunday
1 am
    Brig General Hon F. Gordon
    Commanding 19th Infantry Brigade
        13th June 1915

I anticipated a very happy
time when I took up command
on 5th September, 1914, but it
was not possible to realize
fully then what a high
privilege it would be to
command a Brigade on
Active Service.
    Over nine months have
passed by, and we have lived
through some stirring times
together, but the 19th Infantry
Brigade has eagerly responded
to all calls made upon it.
    On the line of march, in
action and when coping with
the dangers and hardships
trench warfare, the troops
have ever displayed a most
excellent and cheery spirit
which could not be surpas
    While in billets, (I am
proud to say) not one
complaint has ever been

App 4 A1 (Contd)

by the schedule I count on being under my command during the first nine months.

From my heart I thank all ranks for their unfailing devotion to duty, and loyalty to their Regiments.

The command of the 19th Infantry Brigade, with its attached troops, has been a source of unalloyed pride and pleasure, and has enabled me to make a host of friends.

I wish it had been possible to shake hands with every officer, NCO and man of my beloved Brigade. You must take the will for the deed.

With fervent wishes for your future success and future welfare.

Believe your attached comrade

T. Holton [?] Brig General
Commanding 19th Infantry Brigade

P.S. The command of the Brigade passes tomorrow morning to Lieutenant Colonel P.R. Robertson CMG of 1st Bn The Cameronians, who succeeds me on my being transferred to the command of a Division, the 1st Division in England.

"A" Form.
MESSAGES AND SIGNALS.
Army Form C. 2121.

Prefix	Code	m.	Words	Charge	This message is on a/c of:	Recd. at 9.10 a.m.
Office of Origin and Service Instructions			Sent At 10 a.m. To A S D By H Sgt		Service. (Signature of "Franking Officer.")	Date From H Q By

TO — OC Shans S Hrs

Sender's Number	Day of Month	In reply to Number	
A 980	22		A A A

General Robertson much pleased with last nights successful enterprise and useful information obtained aaa Please convey his heartiest congratulations to all who took part

"D" Coy
Repeated.

From
Place
Time

19th Brigade.   Appx A 3.

Report on Reconnaissance carried out on the night of June 21st - 22nd

Reconnaissance by right Company (Section of line 56) to find out whether Trench Sap shown in Aeroplane photograph of June 12th was being continued to form a salient to the enemy's trench, whether any work was being done in it, whether it was strongly held.

Reconnaissance by left Company (Section 58-59) to endeavour to gain the information required by G.H.Q. as to what troops were in front of the right of the 3rd Corps. —

My orders were that both reconnaissances were to be carried out by parties of not less than fifty men. —

The O.C. 11th Battery R.F.A. was asked to lay 2 guns on the enemy's parapet in front of Sections 56 and 59. The Captains of right and left companies were connected up direct with the O.C. Battery. — The O.C. 2nd Welsh Fusiliers and detachment 5th Scottish Rifles were asked to lay a machine gun on parts of the enemy's parapet.

These precautions and the strength of the parties detailed were on account of the late activities in front of the line in the endeavour to gain the information required by G.H.Q. and severe opposition was anticipated. —

"The right Company Reconnaissance was carried out by "B" Coy. Captain Clark who detailed 50 men under 2nd Lieut Bankier to proceed in three parties to the Sap mentioned. — They met with no opposition until the left party arrived close to the Sap when they were challenged and heavily fired on by a party outside the Sap. — The centre and right parties approached the Saps and got round it. It was found that the Saps does not continue any further than what is shown in the photograph, and there is no attempt being made to join it up to the parapet to its left (enemy side). It appeared to be strongly held. An attempt was to have been made to enter the Saps but as the three parties lost touch had to be abandoned. — 2nd Lieut Bankier displayed great coolness and intelligence in conducting the reconnaissance. —

Page 2. Continuance of   Report on Reconnaissance. June 21st - 22nd   Appx a 3 (contd)

Left Company Reconnaissance - was carried out by D Coy Captain Purvis who detailed 50 men under Lieut Aitken to proceed to the enemy's listening post where they had bolted a post of 8 men the previous night. They were to divide in two parties on each side of the gaps leading to the listening post and in the event the post again running away to remain concealed until the enemy patrol came out to investigate. The left of the party lost touch with the right. The right got to its position near the gaps and concealed itself. The left meanwhile got away to its left and came upon a large body of Germans which attacked it and surrounded a party under Sergeant Macpherson who however gallantly fought his way through and brought it eventually back to the breastwork with only two casualties. As the right party under Lieut Aitken was still out and apparently surrounded Sergeant Macpherson with two fresh sections himself armed with two revolvers went out again and fought his way back to Lieut Aitken, driving the Germans before him. Lieut Aitken meanwhile realising that the left party had lost touch with him sent scouts to the left and found Germans retiring. He collected his party to the left and fired on the Germans who made off for their trenches with Lieut Aitken's party in pursuit, when he got the helmet and coat which was thrown away by a hurrying German. Strong German reinforcements now were reported moving on both flanks, and trying to surround Lieut Aitken's party and Sergeant Macpherson's party which had now joined him. Lieut Buchanan was sent out with two sections and did good work in covering the retirement of the patrol. The enemy eventually was driven off and opened a heavy fire from a position in front of their wire. The patrol was by then behind the breastworks.

Casualties were one man killed; one man dangerously wounded; one man missing. The enemy's casualties were heavy. Sergeant Macpherson is known to have accounted for seven.

                                    (Sd) R. L. Gore, Commdg
22-6-15   2nd Argyll & Suth. Highrs

                 Certified true copy.
                                   Capt
                              Adjt S/A S. H.

19th Infantry Brigade.

27th Division.

(Battn. with Bde. joined 2nd Division on 19.8.15)

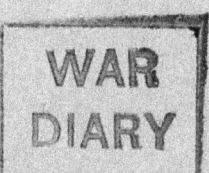

2nd BATTN. THE ARGYLL AND SUTHERLAND HIGHLANDERS.

J U L Y

1 9 1 5

Attached:

Appendices A1, A2, A3 & A4.

Confidential.

War Diary.

2nd Battalion, Argyll & Suth'd High'rs

From 1st July, 1915 to 31st July, 1915.

Army Form C. 2118.

WAR DIARY
of
INTELLIGENCE SUMMARY

(Erase heading not required.)

Instructions regarding War Diaries and Intelligence Summaries are contained in F. S. Regs., Part II. and the Staff Manual respectively. Title pages will be prepared in manuscript.

Hour, Date, Place	Summary of Events and Information	Remarks and references to Appendices
1.7.15, Erio Pot.	In Billets during the day. Took over trenches near Burnt Farm at night. 2 men wounded.	M¹
2.7.15, W¹¹ Rue du Bois	In Trenches, 1 man killed.	M¹
3.7.15 — " —	In Trenches. Notification received that Lieutenants J.C. Aitken and R.G. Moir were awarded the Military Cross.	M¹
4.7.15 — " —	In Trenches 4 men killed and 5 wounded, one of the latter died of wounds same day.	M¹
5.7.15 — " —	In Trenches. Usual routine of trench work.	M¹
6.7.15 — " —	In Trenches during the day. Relieved from the trenches and proceeded to Billets.	M¹
7.7.15 Erio Pot.	In Billets. Notification received that N° 7174 Sergt. W. P. McPherson was awarded the Distinguished Conduct Medal.	M¹

Army Form C. 2118.

WAR DIARY
of
INTELLIGENCE SUMMARY
(Erase heading not required.)

Instructions regarding War Diaries and Intelligence Summaries are contained in F.S. Regs., Part II. and the Staff Manual respectively. Title pages will be prepared in manuscript.

Hour, Date, Place		Summary of Events and Information	Remarks and references to Appendices
8.7.15.	Erie Post. In Billets.	Captain J.L.G. Swine killed, Captain & Adjutant J. Kennedy & Captain H.D. Clark wounded, Severe, 3 men killed and 5 wounded, two of the latter died of wounds the same day. The above casualties were caused by shell fire.	M.A.
9.7.15.	Erie Post. In Billets.	Re-arrangement of Billets.	M.A.
10.7.15.	" " In Billets.	Smoke helmets of Battalion inspected by a medical officer from Field Ambulance, and those that were dry resprayed.	M.A.
11.7.15.	" " In Billets.	Battalion took over the trenches at night — no casualties.	M.A.
12.7.15.	Mt. Rue du Bois. In Trenches.	Usual Routine of trench work.	M.A.

Army Form C. 2118.

WAR DIARY
or
INTELLIGENCE SUMMARY
(Erase heading not required.)

Instructions regarding War Diaries and Intelligence Summaries are contained in F. S. Regs., Part II. and the Staff Manual respectively. Title pages will be prepared in manuscript.

Hour, Date, Place	Summary of Events and Information	Remarks and references to Appendices
13.7.15. M. Rue du Bois	In Trenches Usual Routine of Trench Work.	NA
14.7.15 — " —	In Trenches — do —	NA
15.7.15 — " —	In Trenches. Draft of 20 men joined from Base.	NA
16.7.15 — " —	In Trenches during the day. Proceeded to Billets at La Rolanderie Farm, the Headquarters of the Battalion billeted in Farm. Remainder in the vicinity. 1 man wounded.	NA
17.7.15 La Rolanderie Farm.	In Billets. Notification received that 19th Infantry Brigade would move on Monday 19th to near Le Pt. Mortier.	appx. A.1.
18.7.15 — " —	Divine Service for all denominations.	NA
19.7.15 — " —	Preparing for move. Handing over Billets.	NA
" 3.30 p.m. Erquinghem Road Junction.	March. Moved off in following order Signallers Pipes "A", "B", "C", "D" Coys Machine Guns Stretcher Bearers. First line Transport. Arrive at Billets at 7.30 p.m. Pt. Le Pt. Mortier.	Appx A2

Army Form C. 2118.

WAR DIARY
or
INTELLIGENCE SUMMARY

(Erase heading not required.)

Instructions regarding War Diaries and Intelligence Summaries are contained in F.S. Regs., Part II. and the Staff Manual respectively. Title pages will be prepared in manuscript.

Hour, Date, Place	Summary of Events and Information	Remarks and references to Appendices
20.4.15. Pt Morton	In Billets. Parades.	JA
21.4.15 —	In Billets. Parades.	JA.
22.4.15 —	In Billets. Battalion inspected by Lieut. General Sir W. P. Pulteney, K.C.B., D.S.O. Commⁿᵈᵍ 3rd Corps.	JA Apdx A3
23.4.15 —	In Billets during day, marched to trenches with a halt till dusk at Nouveau Monde, Permissions took over trenches from 2/5 Lancashire Fusiliers. Relief carried out with no casualties.	JA Apdx A4
24.4.15 "	In Trenches. 3 men wounded. Improving trenches.	JA
25.4.15 "	In Trenches. Improving trenches.	JA.
26.4.15 "	In Trenches. Improving trenches. 2ⁿᵈ Lieut. Gillespie reconnoitred the enemy's trenches with a patrol. He succeeded in gaining valuable information as to the enemy's position & defences. He brought back an iron hook (used by the enemy in wire entanglements) who made to screw into the ground.	JA

1247 W 3299 200,000 (E) 8/14 J.B.C. & A. Forms/C. 2118/11.

WAR DIARY
or
INTELLIGENCE SUMMARY
(Erase heading not required.)

Army Form C. 2118.

Instructions regarding War Diaries and Intelligence Summaries are contained in F. S. Regs., Part II. and the Staff Manual respectively. Title pages will be prepared in manuscript.

Hour, Date, Place	Summary of Events and Information	Remarks and references to Appendices
27.7.15 Suicoulin Post	In Trenches. 2 Wounded. Trenches heavily shelled with trench mortars.	MM
28.7.15 " "	In Trenches. Lt. Sir Philip Foster visited the Battalion and had a night round the trenches occupied by the Battalion.	MM
29.7.15 " "	In Trenches. In trenches during the day. Proceeded to Billets in the evening, in the vicinity of Nouveau Monde.	MM
30.7.15 Nouveau Monde In Billets.	Cleaning up.	MM
31.7.15 " "	Physical Training, Company Drill, r Routemarching.	MM

A P P E N D I C E S

    A1
    A2
    A3
    A4

SECRET   B.M./0.3

Officer Commanding
        2/A & S.H.

　　　The Brigade will be relieved on night 19th - 20th
July by 62nd Infantry Brigade and will move to
billeting area in neighbourhood of PETIT MORTIER G.4.
　　　The Brigade will probably go into trenches on
night right of 8th Division about 23rd July.
　　　Please acknowledge by wire.

                                              H E Browne
17/7/16.   Captain,
                              Brigade Major 19th Infantry Brigade.

App 4 B2

Copy No: 5

19th Infantry Brigade Operation Order No: 42

18th July, 1915.

1. The Brigade will be relieved on the night 19th - 20th July, by the 82nd Infantry Brigade; and will move to billets in district West and South West of STEENWERCK (A.17).

2. Details of reliefs will be arranged between battalions concerned, at 19th Infantry Brigade Headquarters at 2.pm today.

3. Battalions will assemble and march to new billetting areas, as per March Table which will be issued later. Billets will be handed over to representatives of relieving units at a time also to be notified later.

4. Regimental transport, except that actually required for baggage from the trenches will move independently under battalion arrangements so as to reach their new lines during daylight.

5. The following trench stores, in addition to ammunition will be handed over to relieving battalions and receipt taken:-

               Picks,
               Shovels,
               Pumps,
               Loopholed plates,
               Braziers,
               Trench boxes,
               Ladders,
               Buckets,
               Sniperscopes,
               Grenades,
               Very's lights,
               Vermorel sprayers.

6. The Sapping Platoons will move with Brigade Headquarters. The parties at present at the Brigade Grenade School will rejoin their units on morning of 20th July.

H.E.Brame
Captain,

Issued at 10.15.am   Brigade Major 19th Infantry Brigade.

Copy No: 1 Filed,
       2 2nd R.W.Fusiliers,
       3 The Cameronians,
       4 1st Middlesex Regt.,
       5 2nd A. & S.Hrs.,
       6 5th Sco.Rifles (Billets)
       7 5th Sco.Rifles (Trenches)
       8 27th Division,
       9 82nd Infantry Brigade,
     10 19th Field Ambulance,
     11 19th Bde.Ammunition Column.
     12 19th Brigade Train,
     13 19th Brigade Supply Column,
     14 Brigade Transport Officer

Appx A2

B.M./D.3

1. Herewith March Table to be attached to Operation Order No: 42 of to day.

The times of starting are arranged to fit in with the crossings of other units and will be strictly adhered to.

2. During daylight no large body of troops will be moved on the roads towards the position of assembly

3. 3 motor ambulances, one for each unit, will be stationed at CROIX DU BAC from 4.pm till 7.pm in case they may be required.

One horse ambulance will be at the position of assembly of each of the trench battalions at 10.30.pm to accompany them on the march. A guide will meet each ambulance on its arrival at battalion billets and conduct it to the 19th Field Ambulance billets.

4. Brigade Headquarters, after reliefs are completed, will be at A.22.a 1.7

5. Please acknowledge receipt by wire.

18/7/15.

Captain,
Brigade Major 19th Infantry Brigade.

Issued with Operation Order No: 42.   MARCH TABLE: 19th Infantry Brigade.

UNIT	Place of assembly and starting point	Time of starting	ROUTE.	Billeting area
2nd Royal Welsh Frs.	Road junction, H.14.a via road junction H.15.c and CROIX DE ROME.	3.15.pm	FORT ROMPU - BAC ST MAUR Bridge - CROIX DU BAC - Pt.VANUXEEM (A.29.8) - le Pt.MORTIER - road junction A.21.d - road junction A.20.a 5.2	All farms on road between Fme du BOIS LA ROSE Fme A.19.A.14.
2nd A. & S. Highlanders	Road junction H.4.d 6.7	3.30.pm	ERQUINGHEM Bridge - cross roads B.27.d - CROIX DU BAC (G.6.c) - Pt.de la BOUDRETTE - road junction G.10.a - road junction G.3.d	Farms in A.28.c.d and G.2.b
Hd.Qrs. and Battn. 5th Sco.Rifles.	Road junction H.5.b 7.6 (not shown on map) reached by road past Brigade H.Q. and track in H.6.d 7.7	3.30.pm	ERQUINGHEM Bridge - cross roads B.27.d - CROIX DU BAC - Pt.VANUXEEM (A.29.c) - le Pt.MORTIER (G.4.a)	Farms on road from A.27.d to A.21.d
The Cameronians	Farm at H.17.d 2.0	On completion of relief.	Road junctions in H.22.b 9.1 and H.16.c - CROIX DE ROME - FORT ROMPU - BAC ST MAUR bridge - CROIX DU BAC - road junction G.5.b - le SEQUEMEAU A.30.c - STEENWERCK - le Gd.BEAUMART A.22.a	Farms on road from A.20.b to A.19.d
1st Middlesex Regiment.	La ROLANDERIE Fme. H.11.c	On completion of relief.	ERQUINGHEM Bridge - cross roads B.27.d - road junction l'HALLOBEAU B.25.c 7.6 - road junction A.18.c 4.2 - STEENWERCK	Farms on road in A.15.a.b.
1 Battn. 5th Sco.Rifles.	Farm at road junction H.11.d 6.5	On completion of relief.	Road junction H.5.d - ERQUINGHEM Bridge - thence by route as for other half Battalion.	Along road from A.27.d to A.21.d

Issued at 7.15.pm
18/7/15.

W.B.Brown Captain,
Brigade Major 19th Infantry Brigade.

Appx. A. 3.

SPEECH OF Lieutenant-General Sir W.P.Pulteney,K.C.B., D.S.O.,Commanding 3rd. Corps.

" Col. Gore,Officers and men of the 2nd.Argyll & Sutherland Highlanders"

I have come here this morning to say a few words to you and let you know how pleased I am to see you as this is the first opportunity I have had of inspecting you since you joined the 3rd.Corps. No regiment had harder work or did better during the early days of the War. I well remember when your Brigade first joined the 3rd.Corps after the fight at Nery ,and what a streneous and difficult task you had in doing rear guard during the remainder of the Retirement.

Since then you have had several hard knocks. After being present at the Battle of the Marne and Ainse you were sent to re-inforce the 7th.Division in Belgium. Then you were sent on a very long march and fought at Fromelles.
You were then sent for a rest but we had to call on you again to go and help in that place the soldiers call "Plug Street"(Ploegsteert). Since then you have had a long and arduous tour of trench duty without any relief,indeed, the only rest you have had was for the short time at Septmonts. I am pleased to hear from Col.Gore that quite a goodly number have come through it all.
After all your hard time and knocks you have pulled yourselves together and I am exceptionally pleased at your excellent appearance ,and splendid health. It does you great credit for it shows how well you have taken care of yourselves.
Your behaviour has been very good and now that you are going to a new part of the line I hope you will keep up your good name and I wish you every success."

SECRET app 4 A4, O/6

WARNING ORDER

Officer Commanding
2/A. & S.H.

The Brigade will relieve the 154th Infantry Brigade (51st Division) on the night 23rd - 24th July.

Detailed orders will be issued later.

21st July, 1915.

J E Browne
Captain,
Brigade Major 19th Infantry Bde.

Appx. A4.

Copy No: 6

19th Infantry Brigade Operation Order No:43

Ref 1/40,000
map, sheet 36.
Sketch map
attached.

22nd July, 1915.

1. The Brigade will relieve the 154th Infantry Brigade (51st Division) and take over the trench line between M.24.b 7.9 and N.8.c 4.7 with the various supporting posts in rear on evening of 23rd July. The above includes the portion of the trench line 50 yards East and West of the FAUQUISSART - TRIVELET road with supporting post E.4 which will be taken over the same night from the SIRHIND Brigade of the Lahore (Indian) Division.

2. (a) The 2nd Royal Welsh Fusiliers will take over part of E lines and part of F lines as far as (X) with supporting posts E.4: F.1: F.2.
   (b) The 2nd Argyll and Sutherland Highlanders will take over the remainder of F. lines with supporting posts F.3: F.4: and F.5.
   (c) The 1st Bn. Middlesex Regiment will be in billets along the RUE DU BACQUEROT (M.17.d to M.6.d) and will find garrisons for second line posts 11, 12, 13, 14, 17 and 18. Post 11 will be taken over from the SIRHIND Brigade.
   (d) The 5th Bn. Scottish Rifles will be in Brigade Reserve in LAVENTIE.
   (e) The 1st Bn. The Cameronians will be in Divisional Reserve in the RUE DE LA LYS.   G.27, G.34.

3. Details of reliefs of E and F lines and 2nd line posts will be arranged between Officers Commanding 2nd Royal Welsh Fusiliers, 2nd A. & S. Highlanders and 1st Bn. Middlesex Regiment and Commanding Officers of outgoing battalions, at the 154th Infantry Brigade Headquarters (G.35.c 6.3) at 2.pm to day.
The Brigade Machine Gun Officer will meet the 154th Infantry Brigade Machine Gun Officer at the same place and time.

4. Further orders with March Table will be issued later.

Captain,

Issued at 8.am

Brigade Major 19th Infantry Brigade.

Copy No: 1 Filed,
   2 Staff Captain,
   3 2nd R.W. Fusiliers,
   4 The Cameronians,
   5 1st Bn. Middlesex Regt.,
   6 2nd A. & S. Highlanders,
   7 5th Scottish Rifles,
   8 19th Field Ambulance,
   9 19th Brigade Amm. Column,
   10 19th Brigade Train,
   11 19th Brigade Supply Column,
   12 Brigade Transport Officer,
   13 H.Q., 8th Division,
   14 H.Q. 154th Inf. Bde.
   15 H.Q. Sirhind Brigade.

Appx A4

Copy No: 6

19th Infantry Brigade After Order
    to be attached to Operation Order No: 43.

Reference 1/40,000 map.
22nd July, 1915.

1. The Battalions of the Brigade will move to-morrow as per March Table attached.

2. The usual trench stores will be taken over. Periscopes, hyposcopes, telescopic rifles, hedging gloves, wire cutters, and catapults are not being handed over by the relieved battalions.

3. Regimental transport will move independently under battalion arrangements.

4. The sapping platoons will move with their regimental transport. The sapping platoon officers will meet the Staff Captain at LAVENTIE Station (M.4.b 0.10) at 3.pm

5. Present Brigade Headquarters will be closed at 6.pm and open at M.4.b 3.5 at the same hour.

Issued at 9.45.pm

H E Browne
Captain,
Brigade Major 19th Infantry Brigade.

Copy No: 1 Filed,
    2 Staff Captain,
    3 2nd R.W.Fusiliers,
    4 The Cameronians,
    5 1st Middlesex Regt.,
    6 2nd A. & S.Highlanders,
    7 5th Scottish Rifles,
    8 19th Field Ambulance,
    9 19th Brigade Amm.Column,
    10 19th Brigade Train,
    11 19th Brigade Supply Column,
    12 Brigade Transport Officer,
    13 H.Q. 8th Division,
    14 H.Q. 154th Infantry Bde.,
    15 H.Q. Sirhind Brigade.

To be attached to Operation Order, No: 43.

MARCH TABLE BATTALIONS 19th INFANTRY BRIGADE

23rd JULY, 1915.

Unit	Starting point.	Time of passing starting point.	ROUTE.	BILLETS.
2nd A. & S. Highlanders.	Road junction, G.9.c 3.9	5.pm.	SAILLY Bridge.	Halt near road junction G.27.d till the evening when battalion will move forward to trenches via M.5.b
2nd Royal Welsh Frs.	Road junction, A.20.a 6.1	10.am	Road junction G.9.c - SAILLY Bridge.	Halt near road junction G.27.d till the evening when battalion will move forward to trenches via G.27.b and LAVENTIE.
1st Middlesex Regiment.	Cross roads, A.23.a	7.45.pm	LE Pt.MORTIER - Pt. de la BOUDRETTE - A.10.d - SAILLY Bridge - road junction G.27.d - to M.5.b	The battalion will be met by guides at 10.pm at road junction M.5.b whence companies will be guided to their billets in Rue du BACQUEROT.
5th Scottish Rifles.	Cross roads at Le Pt.MORTIER G.4.a	7.15.pm	Pt. de la BOUDRETTE - SAILLY Bridge - road junctions at G.27.d and G.34.d	North end of LAVENTIE.
The Cameronians	Road junction A.25.d 2.6	7.30.pm	½ SAILLY Bridge.	Area G.27.b.c and d.

22/7/15.

J. E. Brown
Captain,
Brigade Major 19th Infantry Bde.

App 4 A 4

BATTALION ORDERS
by
LIEUTENANT-COLONEL, R.C.GORE, COMMANDING, 2nd. ARGYLL & SUTHERLAND HIGHLANDERS.

IN THE FIELD, 22nd. JULY, 1915.

1. PROMOTIONS & APPOINTMENTS.

Reference Battalion Order No.10, of yesterday's date, erase the name of No.9441, Sergt. W. Harris. "A" Coy. and the remarks against his name, as this appointment is now cancelled.

No.10442, Sergt. J. Leighton, "D" Coy. is appointed Acting Company Quartermaster Sergeant with effect from 21st. July, 1915.

2. TRANSFERS.

No.10442, A/C.Q.M.S. J. Leighton, "D" Coy. is transferred to "A" Coy. with effect from this date.
No.10631, Sergt. J. McDonald, "A" Coy. is transferred to "D" Coy. with effect from this date.

3. MOVES.

(a) The Battalion will relieve the 2/5th. Lancashire Fusiliers in the trenches near PICANTIN (N 7 b) tomorrow evening, 23rd. July.

(b) The Battalion will march at 3.p.m. by SAILLY - RUE de la LYS - to near road junction (G 27 d) where they will halt for teas.
Companies will pass the starting point road junction (G 2 c) at 3 p.m. in the following order :-
Signallers, Pipers, "B" "C" "D" & "A" Coys., Machine Gun, Transport. Stretcher bearers with their companies.
Companies will march independently to the starting point and form up on road leading from Le Pt MORTIER.
Transport can go to starting point by shortest road and join column after it is on the march.

(c) TRANSPORT. One wagon will collect blankets and officers trench kit from "A" & "B" Coys. and Hd.Qrs., and one wagon from "C" & "D" Coys. and Machine Gun starting at 1.30.p.m.
BLANKETS again will be issued after teas.
COOKERS will accompany Battalion for teas.
VALISES. One wagon will collect officers valises starting from Machine Gun & "D" Coy. at 12.noon.
Orders for remainder of 2nd. Line Transport and S.A.A. carts will be issued later.
HAND CARTS to follow wagons on line of march.

(d) RATIONS for 24th will be issued and carried by the men
FUEL being put on the wagons and afterwards transferred to the hand carts.

(e) TRENCHES The Battalion will take up the trenches in the following order from right to left - "A" "B" "C" & "D" Coys.
O.C. Coys. and Machine Gun Officer will rendezvous at Lancashire Fusiliers Head Quarters (M 6 d 5 e) at 4.30p.m. and will take over their trenches in advance.
Method of proceeding to the trenches will be explained to O.C. Coys.

(f) TELEPHONES. There are telephones to each Coy. from Battalion Head Quarters. Signallers will be sent on in advance under orders from Adjutant.

(g) AID POST is near road junction (M 6 d 5 5).

(Sd) H.H.G. HYSLOP, MAJOR,
A/ADJUTANT, 2nd. ARGYLL & SUTHERLAND HIGHLANDERS.

2ND DIVISION
19TH INFY BDE

2ND BATTALION ARGYLL & SUTHERLAND HDRS.
AUG - NOV 1915.

To 33 DIV 98 BDE

W.13.

19th Infantry Brigade.
2nd Division.

(Battn. with Bde left
2) 2 Div. 19.8.15)

WAR DIARY

2nd BATTN. THE ARGYLL & SUTHERLAND HIGHLANDERS.

A U G U S T

1 9 1 5

Attached:

Appendices A.1 to A.6.

(CONFIDENTIAL)

WAR DIARY.

2nd. BATTALION, ARGYLL & SUTHERLAND HIGHLANDERS.

From 1st. August, 1915 to 31st. August, 1915.

WAR DIARY
or
INTELLIGENCE SUMMARY
(Erase heading not required.)

Army Form C. 2118.

Instructions regarding War Diaries and Intelligence Summaries are contained in F. S. Regs., Part II. and the Staff Manual respectively. Title Pages will be prepared in manuscript.

Place	Date	Hour	Summary of Events and Information	Remarks and references to Appendices
NOUVEAU MONDE	1.8.15		In Billets. Divine Service.	AmB
"	2.8.15		In Billets. Physical Drill, Training, Baths.	AmB
"	3.8.15		In Billets. — do — — do — — do —	AmB
"	4.8.15		In Billets. — do — — do — — do —	AmB
			Moved to Billets in Laventie in Evening.	
LAVENTIE	5.8.15		In Billets. Fitting clothing and preparing for taking over Trenches.	AmB
"	6.8.15		In Billets. during the day. Took over trenches at night- near Picantui. 1 man slightly wounded.	AmB
PICANTIN	7.8.15		In Trenches. 1 Man dangerously wounded. Trenches which was in a poor state of defence when taken over, being put- in a proper state.	AmB
"	8.8.15		In Trenches. 2 Lance Corporals of the Battalion were out between the two lines of trenches burying a dead body. They discovered two Germans whom they attacked and succeeded, after a hand to hand fight, in capturing one of them. The others were unarmed.	AmB Appx A.1.

1875. Wt. W593/826 1,000,000 4/15 J.B.C. & M. A.D.S.S./Forms/C. 2118.

WAR DIARY or INTELLIGENCE SUMMARY

Army Form C. 2118

(Erase heading not required.)

Place	Date	Hour	Summary of Events and Information	Remarks and references to Appendices
(Picantin) PICANTIN	9.8.15		In Trenches. Improving trenches. 1 man seriously wounded, who subsequently died of his wounds.	Aut
"	10.8.15		In Trenches. Improving trenches.	Aut3
"	11.8.15		In Trenches. Improving trenches. 1 man wounded.	Aut
"	12.8.15		In Trenches, during the day. Evacuated trenches in the evening "A" & "C" Cos. proceeding to Billets in LAVENTIE and "B" & "D" Cos. in Reserve at RUE DU BACQUEROT.	Aut
"	13.8.15		In Billets ½ Battalion in Billets and ½ Battalion in Reserve. 1 Sergeant wounded returning with a party which was digging at the Trenches.	Aut
"	14.8.15		" " ½ Battalion in Billets and ½ Battalion in Reserve.	Aut
"	15.8.15		" " Divine Service.	Aut3
"	16.8.15		In Billets during day. Moved off to new Billeting Area. Left 8 p.m. Bivouac. Congratulatory Message received for good work done while attached to 8th Division.	Appx A 2. Appx A 3. Aut

Army Form C. 2118.

WAR DIARY
or
INTELLIGENCE SUMMARY

(Erase heading not required.)

Hour, Date, Place	Summary of Events and Information	Remarks and references to Appendices
17.8.15, Vieux Berquin	In Billets. Physical Training & Drill.	AppxB.
18.8.15, " —	In Billets. — do —	AppxB.
19.8.15, " —	In Billets availed ofband. Marched to BETHUNE marched parts to join 2nd Division. Lord Kitchener on line of march.	Appx A.4. AppxB. Appx A.5.
20.8.15 BETHUNE	In Billets. Physical Training and Drill.	AppxB.
21.8.15 " —	In Billets. Lieut. J.L. Bullough joined Battalion.	AppxB.
22.8.15 " —	In Billets. Lieutenants J.D.Fordyce, J.C. Fraser, J.F. Fraser joined Battalion.	AppxB.
23.8.15 " —	In Billets. Physical Training & Drill.	AppxB.
24.8.15 " —	In Billets during the morning. Moved to take over trenches at 12.30 p.m. at GUINCHY. Relief carried out without any casualties.	Appx A.6.

Army Form C. 2118.

WAR DIARY
INTELLIGENCE SUMMARY
(Erase heading not required.)

Hour, Date, Place		Summary of Events and Information	Remarks and references to Appendices
25.8.15	ORCHARD REDOUBT	In Trenches.	
26.8.15	"	In Trenches, 2 men killed, and 4 wounded.	AmB
27.8.15	"	In Trenches. 1 man killed and 2 wounded.	AmB
28.8.15	"	In Trenches, till about 3 P.M. when relieved by 5th Scottish Rifles. No casualties occurred during the relief. Proceeded to Billets at BEUVRY.	AmB
29.8.15	BEUVRY.	In Billets. Physical Training and drill.	AmB
30.8.15	"	In Billets. — do — — do —	AmB
31.8.15	"	In Billets. Lieut. C. C. G. Johnstone rejoined Battalion.	AmB

AmB Bankier Lieut
a/Adjt 9th Argyll & Suth. Highrs

A P P E N D I C E S

A.1
A.2
A.3
A.4
A.5
A.6

APPENDIX. A 1.

Extract from Routine Orders by Lieutenant General, Sir, W.P.Pulteney, K.C.B., D.SO., Commanding, 3rd. Corps, dated, 13th. August, 1915:-

" The Corps Commander has much pleasure in bringing the
" following act to notice:- "

" On the 8th. of August, 2 Lance Corporals of the
" 2nd. Battalion, Argyll & Sutherland Highlanders, were in
" front of the trenches burying a dead body. They saw two
" Germans to their left front and went forward to capture
" them. A hand to hand struggle ensued, one German escap-
" ing, and the other showing fight. The latter was captured
" and brought in. Both sides were unarmed. "

Certified true extract.

AmBankie,   Lieutenant,

15-8-15.   A/ADJUTANT, 2nd. ARGYLL & SUTHERLAND HIGHRS.

Appy. A 2.

SECRET Copy No: 6

19th Infantry Brigade Operation Order No: 44

Ref. 1/40,000 maps,
Sheets 36, 36 A. 14th August, 1915.

1. The Brigade will be relieved by the 59th Infantry Brigade (20th Division) on the nights 15th – 16th and 16th – 17th August as per March Tables attached.
The Brigade will be billeted in area VIEUX BERQUIN – NEUF BERQUIN – DOULIEU (F.7 and 30 and L.8) till 19th August when it will march to 1st Corps area to replace the 4th (Guards') Brigade in the 2nd Division.

2. The Train, Supply Column, Ammunition Column and Field Ambulance will remain in their present billets till 19th August.

3. The Officers Commanding 2nd Royal Welsh Fusiliers and 1st Middlesex Regiment will arrange details of relief with the Officers Commanding 11th Rifle Brigade and 11th K.R.R.C. respectively at Brigade Headquarters at 11.am to-morrow 15th August. Officers Commanding remaining units will meet at same place and time on Monday 16th August.

4. Billeting parties and regimental transports will move under Battalion arrangements. Time of starting to be reported, for approval, to Brigade Headquarters. They can move by daylight – route SAILLY Bridge.

5. Lists showing S.A.A., Hand Grenades and Trench Stores, etc. to be handed over have been issued to units concerned.

6. Sapping platoons will march with and be billeted with, Brigade Headquarters. Parties at the Brigade Grenade School will report to their units at 10.am to-morrow.

7. After reliefs are completed on night of 16th – 17th August, Brigade Headquarters will be at BLEU, F.19.b

Major,

Issued at 10.pm Brigade Major 19th Infantry Brigade.

Copy No: 1 File
2 Staff Captain,
3 2nd R.W.Fusiliers,
4 1st Cameronians
5 1st Middlesex Regt.
6 2nd A. & S.Hrs.
7 5th Scottish Rifles
8 Brigade Transport Officer
9 19th Bde. Train
10 19th Bde. Supply Column
11 19th Bde. Amm.Column
12 19th Field Ambulance
13 H.Q. 8th Division
14 H.Q. 20th Division.
15 H.Q. 59th Inf.Bde.

App 4 A 3.

G 388/K 14/8/15.

3rd Corps.

As the 19th Infantry Brigade are shortly leaving this division I take the opportunity of bringing to the notice of Corps Commander the excellent work performed by them. The defences of the section of the line held by them was by no means satisfactory. They have however put in a great amount of work and the leave the line in a much stronger condition than when they took it over. This is all the more creditable because they well knew that their period of stay in this division was a matter of days only.

14/8/15. (Sd) H.Hudson, Major General,
Commanding 8th Division.

19th Infantry Brigade.

In forwarding the attached copy of a letter received from the G.O.C. 8th Division, the Corps Commander wishes me to convey to you his great appreciation of the work done by the 19th Infantry Brigade.

15/8/15. (Sd) C.F.Romer, Brig.General,
General Staff 3rd Corps.

Officer Commanding
c/a,s,H

In forwarding the above the G.O.C. directs me to say that he considers the praise thoroughly well deserved by the battns. under his command. He never doubted that they would thoroughly carry out, as they have always done, all work required of them and he congratulates them on the fact that their excellent work has been appreciated by higher authority. He desires to thank all ranks for upholding the high reputation gained by the Brigade during its attachment to the 8th Division.

18/8/15.

Major,
Brigade Major 19th Infantry Brigade.

App A4,

MARCH ORDER No: 45   Copy No: 6

19th INFANTRY BRIGADE.

Ref. 1/40,000 squared map (3rd edition)
and 1/100,000 HAZEBROUCK Sheet 5 A.

18th August, 1915.

1. The Brigade will march into billets in and near BETHUNE to-morrow 19th August as per attached March Table.
A halt for dinners will be made at the farm 300 yards N. of AIRE - LA BASSEE Canal (Q.34.c and d).
On receipt of further orders to continue the march, battalions will move forward in the following order:-

    2nd Battn. Argyll and Sutherland Highlanders,
    1st Battn. The Middlesex Regiment.
    1st Battn. The Cameronians.
    2nd Battn. Royal Welsh Fusiliers,
    5th Scottish Rifles.

During the second half of the march, the Brigade will march past Lord Kitchener at the Windmill ½ mile South of HINGES Cross roads.

2. 1st line transport will accompany units. All other transport will march with the Brigade Train. They will be ready loaded at regimental centres not later than 7.30.am.

3. The Sapping Platoons will be at road junction W.N.W. of N of NEUF BERQUIN (L.13.a. 10.8.) at 7.10.am and join their respective units there. They will be billeted and rationed by their own units until further orders.

4. O.C. 19th Field Ambulance will send 3 horse ambulances to be at Brigade starting point at 7.45.am. They will follow in rear of the Brigade.
In addition 2 motor ambulances will be at farm 600 yards N. of AIRE - LA BASSEE Canal (Q.34.c. 6.2) at 10.am

5. The Brigade Train and 19th Field Ambulance will move independently to BETHUNE under their own arrangements.
Route: LA GORGUE - LESTREM - LOCON.

6. Separate orders have been issued to the Brigade Supply Column and Brigade Ammunition Column. They will leave the Brigade to-morrow.

7. Brigade Headquarters during the march will be at the head of the column; afterwards in Rue GAMBETTA, BETHUNE.

Issued at 6.pm

                                    Major,
Brigade Major 19th Infantry Brigade.

Copy No: 1 Office
        2 Staff Captain,
        3 2nd R.W.Fusiliers,
        4 The Cameronians
        5 1st Middlesex Regt.
        6 2nd A. & S.Hrs.
        7 5th Sco.Rifles.
        8 Bde. Transport Officer
        9 Bde Supply Column.
      10 Bde. Ammunition Column
      11 Brigade Train.
      12.Lieut.Stanway (O.C.Sapping Platoons)
      13 H.Q. 2nd Division.
      14 8th Division.

To be attached to March Order No: 45.

MARCH TABLE - 19th INFANTRY BRIGADE

19th AUGUST, 1915.

UNIT.	Starting point	Time of passing starting point	Distance from starting point to BETHUNE.	Approximate distance from billets to starting point	ROUTE	BILLETS	REMARKS.
1st Middlesex Regiment.	road junc. C.13.b. 7.8. 1/40,000 map HAZEBROUCK - MERVILLE - LA BASSEE - AIRE BLN. VIII	7.30.am		1½ miles	MERVILLE - PACAUT -	BETHUNE	1st Middlesex Regiment 2nd R.W.Frs. and 1st Cameronians will reach starting point via Rue PAUVOST (L.8.)
2nd R.Welsh Fusiliers.		7.37.am	} 10 miles	2½ miles	Cross Roads, South of LE CORNET MALO	BETHUNE	
The Cameronians		7.44.am		4 miles	N of LE CORNET MALO	BETHUNE	2nd A. & S.Hrs and 5th Sco.Rifles via -A- COULONNE. (E.30.a)
2nd A. & S. Highlanders		7.51.am		4 miles	HINGES - Cross Roads	BETHUNE	
5th Scottish Rifles		7.58.am	9½ miles (to VERDIN)	4½ miles	South of G of OBLINGHEM	VERDIN - LEZ BETHUNE (M.27.c)	

NOTE: Midday halt for dinners at 300 yards North of AIRE - LA BASSEE Canal (Q.34.c.) 6½ miles from starting point.

Halts. The column will halt for 10 minutes on head reaching:-

1. N. end of MERVILLE
2. PACAUT.

18/8/15.

W.E. Browne (signature)
Major,
Brigade Major 19th Infantry Brigade.

Inspections   Appx A 5.
                                                     Misc. 48

Officer Commanding
    2/A & S Hrs

  After the march past during the march into
Bethune on 19th August, Lord Kitchener expressed his
pleasure at what he had seen of the Brigade. He asked
the Brigadier General to inform the troops that he was
particularly struck with their physique, appearance,
march discipline and general turn out and added that
he considered it to be a very fine Brigade indeed.
Will you please make known these remarks to all ranks
serving under your command.

21/8/15.
                  Major,
             Brigade Major 19th Infantry Bde.

SECRET.   Copy No: 6

appx A 6

19th Infantry Brigade Operation Order No: 46.

23rd August, 1915.

Ref.trench map, and
1/40,000 BETHUNE Sheet.

1. The Brigade will relieve the 6th Infantry Brigade in Section A (CUINCHY) to-morrow 24th August, as per attached Table "A."

2. The sapping platoons will rejoin Brigade Headquarters and be billeted at ANNEQUIN F.23.d.

3. The Brigade Machine Guns will take over machine gun positions to-morrow morning under separate instructions issued through the Brigade Machine Gun Officer.

4. Supporting batteries of 34th brigade R.F.A. are as follows:-

   For A.1: 70th battery, R.F.A.)
   For A.2: 50th battery, R.F.A.) all 18 pdrs.
   For A.3: 18th battery, R.F.A.)

56th howitzer battery is also in communication with all battalion Headquarters in front line and can be called upon direct by battalions for assistance or retaliation.

Further assistance from Heavy Artillery can be given if application is made, through the affiliated field battery, to 34th brigade R.F.A., repeating to Brigade Headquarters.

5. Transport, except such 1st line and officers' kits as accompanies units, will be billeted in BEUVRY.

6. Brigade Headquarters will close at Rue GAMBETTA, BETHUNE, at 5.pm and open at same time at CAMBRIN A.19.d.7.3.

Issued at 5.pm

                                    Major,
                   Brigade Major 19th Infantry Brigade.

Copy No: 1. Office,
        2. Staff Captain,
        3. 2nd Bn.Royal Welsh Fusiliers,
        4. 1st Cameronians,
        5. 1st Bn.Middlesex Regt.,
        6. 2nd Bn.A. & S.Highlanders,
        7. 5th Bn. Scottish Rifles (T)
        8. Captain Stanway and Bde.Sapping Platoons,
        9. H.Q. 6th Infantry Brigade.
      10. H.Q. 2nd Division,
      11. Brigade Transport Officer.

To be attached to Operation Order No: 46.

MARCH TABLE, 19th INFANTRY BRIGADE.

Table "A".

Unit	Battn. to be relieved.	Section of front & posts, or billets.	Rendezvous	Time of arrival of leading platoons.	Approximate number of miles from billets to rendezvous.	Route.	REMARKS.
2nd Battn. R.W. Fusiliers	1st Bn. Royal Berks Regt.	A.2 and The KEEP - The HOLLOW - LOVERS REDOUBT	A.19.d.6.2	3.pm	5¼	BEUVRY - ANNEQUIN.	
	1st Bn. King's Regt.	A.3 and ORCHARD REDOUBT	North end of PONT FIXE A.14.a.10.3	3.pm	5¾	Road junction E.11.b.5.8.- le QUESNOY road junction F.14.b.6.9 - to PREO. bridge F.10.c.8.0 - Vauxhall bridge A.13.b.4.4.	Vauxhall bridge is not shown on map. Battn. crosses to North bank of canal by it. March by Companies at 400 yards distance to road junction F.14.B.6.9 thence by platoons at 100 yards distance.
1st Battn. Camoronians.	1st K.R.R.C	A.1 and PARK LANE REDOUBT, STAFFORD REDOUBT, CAMBRIN Post.	A.19.d.6.2	4.pm	5⅝	BEUVRY - ANNEQUIN.	
1st Battn. Middlesex Regiment.	2nd S.Staff. Regiment.	Billet in ANNEQUIN (2¾ companies) BRADDELL Post - CANTERS Redoubt - TOURBIERES Redoubt - CUINCHY Post (1¼ companies).	F.29.b.4.6	4.30.pm	4½	BEUVRY - ANNEQUIN.	
5th Battn. Sc.Rifles.	1st Herts. Regiment.	Billets in BEUVRY.	F.14.c.0.4	4.45.pm	3½	BETHUNE - BEUVRY.	
Sapping platoons. (O.C.Captain Stanway.)	6th Brigade Grenadier Company.	ANNEQUIN.	F.29.a.4.9	5.15.pm	4½	BEUVRY	Platoons will assemble at Bde.H.Q.,Rue GAMBETTA at 3.pm.

Note. Battalions will march by companies at 400 yards distance to BEUVRY, thence by platoons at 100 yards distance. If shelling takes place platoons will open out by sections.
Guides for each platoon and each redoubt or post will meet platoons and post garrisons at the rendezvous.

28/8/15.

A.D.Biddulph
Major,
Brigade Major 19th Infantry Brigade.

19th Infantry Brigade.
2nd Division.

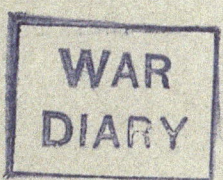

2nd BATTN. THE ARGYLL AND SUTHERLAND HIGHLANDERS.

SEPTEMBER

1915

Confidential

Original

War Diary.

of

2nd Battalion, Argyll & Sutherland Highrs.

From 1st September, 1915, to 30th September, 1915.

INTELLIGENCE SUMMARY

(Erase heading not required.)

Summaries are contained in F.S. Regs., Part II. and the Staff Manual respectively. Title Pages will be prepared in manuscript.

Place	Date	Hour	Summary of Events and Information	Remarks and references to Appendices
BEUVRY	1.9.15		In Billets during morning	N.S.
N⁰. CAMBRIN	1.9.15	2 p.m.	In Trenches - Moved to CAMBRIN to take over trenches. One man killed.	N.S.
- do -	2.9.15		In Trenches - During 2 Germans of the 16th Prussian Regiment came in who gave valuable information about the enemy's position.	N.S.
- do -	3.9.15		In Trenches - Lieut E. W. Glass and five men wounded.	N.S.
- do -	4.9.15		In Trenches during forenoon. Evacuated trenches in the afternoon and proceeded to Billets at BETHUNE.	N.S.
BETHUNE	5.9.15		In Billets - Divine Service, and General cleaning up. Received instructions to move to Billets north of the Canal on the 6th September, 1915.	N.S.

INTELLIGENCE SUMMARY

(Erase heading not required.)

Summaries are contained in F. S. Regs, Part II. and the Staff Manual respectively. Title Pages will be prepared in manuscript.

Place	Date	Hour	Summary of Events and Information	Remarks and references to Appendices
ESSARS	6.9.15		In Billets. Paraded marched to ESSARS, and Billets very scattered.	Nil
-do-	7.9.15	"	Parades. Control of Rapid Fire, Work in extended orders, especially advances in great depth, and forming echelon to a flank, Section leading & Platoon leading. Inspection of Smoke Helmets by C.O. & M.O.	Nil
-do-	8.9.15	"	Parades as above - Hot Baths to 40 men per Company	Nil
-do-	9.9.15	"	Parades as above, also rifle practice on range for indifferent shots. Lieut. C.C.G. Thurston to 1st/13th London Regt.	Nil
-do-	10.9.15	"	Packs marked in indelible pencil with Regt. No. Rank & Name of Owner and number of Platoon as in case of an attack being made packs were to be left behind. Parades.	Nil
-do-	11.9.15	"	Parades & Physical drill.	Nil
-do-	12.9.15	"	Divine Service, Holy Communion.	Nil

INTELLIGENCE SUMMARY

(Erase heading not required.)

Place	Date	Hour	Summary of Events and Information	Remarks and references to Appendices
ESSARS.	13.9.15		In Billets during forenoon, packing up and preparing for removal.	N/S
Nr. LE PREOL	" "		Moved to Billets near LE PREOL.	N/S
— do —	14.9.15		Parades. Battalion furnished parties for mining, in two Reliefs.	N/S
— do —	15.9.15		Reinforcements arrived from Base (15) Men who went down return through wounds & sickness. Parades etc,	N/S
— do —	16.9.15		Parades, Drill & Physical training.	N/S
— do —	17.9.15		In Billets during forenoon.	N/S
Nr. CAMBRIN	" "	3 pm	In Trenches. Taking over Trenches. One man killed.	N/S
"	18.9.15		No Casualties. Heavy Bombardment on our right —	N/S
"	19.9.15		Two men wounded, in the late afternoon.	N/S
"	20.9.15		Two men wounded,	N/S
Nr. BETHUNE	"		In trenches in the forenoon — one man wounded. In Billets. Removed to Billets near Bethune in the afternoon.	N/S

INTELLIGENCE SUMMARY

(Erase heading not required.)

Summaries are contained in F.S. Regs., Part II. and the Staff Manual respectively. Title Pages will be prepared in manuscript.

Place	Date	Hour	Summary of Events and Information	Remarks and references to Appendices
BETHUNE	21.9.15		In Billets. Heavy Bombardment on our front by British.	Nil
- do -	22.9.15		In Billets. Reinforcement (20) arrived from Base.	Nil
- do -	23.9.15		In Billets during morning, proceeded to trenches near Cambrin in the afternoon. Packs & blankets stored in Bethune.	Nil
- do -			In Trenches. Four men wounded.	Nil
CAMBRIN	24.9.15			Nil
- do -	25.9.15		In Trenches - Attack on September 25th, 1915, near CAMBRIN. The ground between our trenches and the Germans was flat except where a series of mines had been exploded which made craters with sides 8 to 9 feet high completely screening the German trenches except for a gap of about 60 yards; one crater known as "Etna" touched our lines, one side of which had been held by us and the other by the Germans for some months. The wire in the gap had been previously cut by our Artillery, and the assault had to pass through this gap to reach the German trenches. This distance across was about 80 yards.	Nil

Place	Date	Hour	Summary of Events and Information	Remarks and references to Appendices
CAMBRIN	25/9/15		Attack on 25th Sept, 1915 (contd)	

The previous night was mild and damp. During the night the wire in front of the parapet, in front of our "jumping off" trenches was removed and bridges laid across the front trench for the attack to get over the parapet which was encumbered with chlorine gas cylinders. Two jumping off trenches had been dug some days previously about 30 to 40 yards in rear of the fire trench, one between Boyau (communicating trenches) 18–19 and one between 17–18, each about 80 yards long. 40 short scaling ladders were in position in each trench. Two companies had two platoons formed up in these "jumping off" trenches, one platoon standing at the ladders the other platoon standing beside the ladders, the two other platoons of these companies were formed up in the support trenches known as "High Street". The orders for the advance were for the platoons at the ladders to lead, followed by the other platoons waiting at the ladders as soon as the leading platoons had cleared the fire trench, followed by the two platoons in High Street in succession.

The other two companies to take these positions as they became vacated.

(Contd)

Place	Date	Hour	Summary of Events and Information	Remarks and references to Appendices
CAMBRIN	25/9/15		The two leading companies were "D" on the left, Captain H. de B. Purves, "B" on the right, Lieut. H.K. Campbell. "B" Company, 3rd Company Captain J.C. Aitken. "C" Company, Captain Wardalo, Ramsay in Reserve. Captain J.C. The Artillery opened fire and 5.50 the gas was turned on at 5.45 am, the artillery opened fire combined with smoke for 40 minutes, the last 5 minutes combined with smoke. At 6.30 am the assault started, the morning being very still, the gas hung about and was inclined to come back which hampered the leading platoons. No 16 Platoon "D" Company Lieut. Bullough, and No 5 Platoon, "B" Company 2nd Lieut. Gillespie advanced and succeeded in reaching the German front trench, on the appearance of the assaulting parties the Germans opened a heavy machine gun and shrapnel fire, 1 more platoon of "B" Company succeeded in crossing the fire trench but were unable to reach the German trenches also support the leading Platoons owing to the heaviness of the fire, the remaining platoons were unable to cross the fire trench, "B" Company endeavoured to cross but were also unable to make any headway. The machine guns came into action under Lieut. Macpherson to support the advance, but could not make no impression (contd)	NI

INTELLIGENCE SUMMARY

(Erase heading not required.)

Place	Date	Hour	Summary of Events and Information	Remarks and references to Appendices
CAMBRIN	25/9/15		on the enemy's fire. The supporting Batteries fired rapid shrapnel but were hampered by the closeness of the 2 lines. As no advance was possible the platoon in front returned to our lines and further attempt was abandoned. Of the two platoons that reached the German trench 11 returned in the evening. Lieut. Bullough was seen to fall and the Germans were and Lieut. Gillespie on the German parapet. Sergt. McLure and about 10 men of 5" Platoon were seen to jump into the German trench, the remainder of them 2 Platoons were "wiped out". Casualties:— Officers:— Captain S. Caulfeild, Killed. Captain A.B. Wardlaw-Ramsay, Wounded. Capt. J.C. Bullough, missing believed killed. Lieut. E.P. Buchanan, Wounded. Lieut. J.M. Miller, Killed. Lieut. A. McPherson, Wounded. Lieut. E.E. Smith, Killed. Lieut. J.Y. Fraser, Wounded. Lieut. H. Kerr, Killed. Lieut. J.R. Bogie, Wounded. Lieut. W.G. Tullowfield, Killed. Lieut. A.S. Gillespie, missing believed killed. Lieut. J.C. Fraser, Killed. Lieut. W.R. Kennedy, Killed. Lieut. J.D. Fordyce, Wounded & died of wounds. Rank & File, 313.	

INTELLIGENCE SUMMARY

(Erase heading not required)

Place	Date	Hour	Summary of Events and Information	Remarks and references to Appendices
CAMBRIN	25/9/15		List of Officers present at the attack on 25th September, 1915:—	

Lieut-Col. R.C. Gore.
Major H.G. Hyslop, D.S.O.
Captain H.A.B Penney.
"   A.B. Wardlaw Ramsay.
"   D.C. Aitken.
Lieut. J.G. Bullough.
"   H.A. Campbell.
"   E.G. Buchanan.
"   J.M. McIlov.
Lieut-Adjt. R.M. Bannier.
Lieut. R.G. Mori. W: C French Mortar Battery
Lieut. G.E. Smith.
Lieut. D.J. Grant.
Lieut. R.S. Gillespie.
2Lieut. H. Kerr.
Lieut. A. McPherson.
2Lieut W.G. Fallowfield Sapping Platoon

2Lieut. R. Bogie
2Lieut. J.O. Fordyce
2Lieut. W.H. Kennedy.
2Lieut. K.C. Fraser.
2Lieut. J.T. Fraser.
2Lieut. J.F. Fraser, R.A.M.C.
Lieut. R.M.C. Hill R.A.M.C.

INTELLIGENCE SUMMARY

(Erase heading not required.)

Hour, Date, Place	Summary of Events and Information	Remarks and references to Appendices
25-9-15. CAMBRIN Sn Trenches (Cntn)	Conspicuous deed of Gallantry:- No. 7844 Sergeant A. Kiddle showed conspicuous bravery in the attack. When a machine gun team which had been pushed forward to assist the assault had been "knocked out" he went out from the fire trench under a heavy fire machine gun fire, brought the gun back and brought it into action. He again went out and brought in 2 wounded men of the team. He was wounded later in the day.	

INTELLIGENCE SUMMARY

(Erase heading not required.)

Hour, Date, Place		Summary of Events and Information	Remarks and references to Appendices
25.9.15 (contd)	CAMBRIN	In trenches. 2 Lieut. D. Biggert joined Battalion and remained with 2nd line transport.	NY
26.9.15	– do –	In trenches. Collecting casualties.	NY
27.9.15.	– do –	Reinforcements joined. 200 N.C.Os & men from Entrenching Battalion and 50 from Base = 250. Proceeded to trenches at night.	NY
		In trenches during day. 4 men killed and 13 wounded. Reinforcements from Base joined = 20 men. Proceeded to Sailly in the evening at Annequin promoting new	NY
28.9.15	ANNEQUIN	In Sailly. General Cleaning up. N.C.Os to complete Establishment, Vacancies caused through Casualties on 26th & heat. N.C.Os being heavily represented in casualties.	NY
29.9.15	– do –	In Sailly. Cleaning up. and	NY
30.9.15	– do –	In Sailly – during forenoon. Proceeded to trenches in afternoon, took over trenches Mr Cauchin from 1st Camerons. no casualties 2nd Lieut. J. O. Mackellar joined.	NY

M Burges 2Lt ?/Adj 2/A.S.Highrs
?-10-1915

19th Infantry Brigade.
2nd Division.

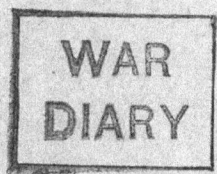

2nd BATTN. THE ARGYLL & SUTHERLAND HIGHLANDERS.

OCTOBER

1915

Confidential.

War Diary

of

2nd Bn. Arg: Suth: Highlanders

From 1st October, 1915, to 31st October, 1915.

WAR DIARY OF INTELLIGENCE SUMMARY

Army Form C. 2118

Hour, Date, Place	Summary of Events and Information	Remarks and references to Appendices
1st October, 1915, CAMBRIN	In trenches, during day, proceeded to Billets in MANNEQUIN. 2nd Lieut. A. B. Lyon joined.	Appx B
2nd October, 1915, MANNEQUIN	In Billets - Cleaning up.	Appx B
3rd October 1915 – do –	In Billets - Moved to Billets in BETHUNE	Appx B
4th October 1915, BETHUNE	In Billets - Parades etc.	Appx B
5th October 1915 – do –	In Billets - Parades etc.	Appx B
6th October 1915, BETHUNE	In Billets - The following officers joined the Battalion:- 2nd Lieut. J. Buchan, 2nd Lieut. R. E. Allan, 2nd Lieut. J. M. Garlick, 2nd Lieut. F. D. Allan, 2nd Lieut. A. Henderson, 2nd Lieut. K. E. McCallum, 2nd Lieut. J. H. Tait, 2nd Lieut. H. S. Smith. 280 N.C.Os and men joined as a reinforcement from Base. In Billets - Parades etc.	Appx B

Army Form C. 2118.

WAR DIARY
or
INTELLIGENCE SUMMARY

(Erase heading not required.)

Instructions regarding War Diaries and Intelligence Summaries are contained in F. S. Regs., Part II. and the Staff Manual respectively. Title pages will be prepared in manuscript.

Hour, Date, Place	Summary of Events and Information	Remarks and references to Appendices
7th October, 1915, BETHUNE	In Billets:- Parades etc:	AWB
8th October, 1915 — do —	In Billets:- 2nd Lieut. K. A. Kennedy & D. Campbell joined Battalion. Parades etc.	AWB
9th October, 1915 — do —	In Billets:- Parades etc 2nd Lieut. E. C. Moatelyne joined Battalion.	AWB
10th October, 1915 — do —	In Billets:- Sunday - Divine Service.	AWB
11th October, 1915 — do —	In Billets:- Battalion by Companies practising attack on trenches.	AWB
12th October, 1915 — do —	In Billets:- — do — 2nd Lieut. A. G. Stirling joined.	AWB
13th October, 1915 — do —	In Billets:- Battalion Drill. 2nd Lieut. J. M. Keren joined.	AWB

WAR DIARY
INTELLIGENCE SUMMARY
(Erase heading not required.)

Army Form C. 2118.

Instructions regarding War Diaries and Intelligence Summaries are contained in F.S. Regs., Part II. and the Staff Manual respectively. Title pages will be prepared in manuscript.

Hour, Date, Place	Summary of Events and Information	Remarks and references to Appendices
14th October, 1915 BETHUNE In Billets.	Battalion Parade - Practice "Advance in Artillery Formation."	AWB
15th " " " In Billets.	— do —	AWB
16th " " " In Billets.	Morning; proceeded to take over trenches near Cambrin at 8.30 a.m.	AWB
CAMBRIN In Trenches	3 men wounded.	AWB
17th " " " In Trenches	Improving trenches, one man killed, one man wounded.	AWB
18th " " " In Trenches	Improving trenches, Two men wounded.	AWB
19th " " " In Trenches	Improving trenches. Five men wounded	AWB
20th " " " In Trenches	during day. 3 men wounded.	AWB
— " " ANNEQUIN In Billets	Settling down to Billets in the afternoon.	AWB

Army Form C. 2118.

WAR DIARY
or
INTELLIGENCE SUMMARY

(Erase heading not required.)

Instructions regarding War Diaries and Intelligence Summaries are contained in F. S. Regs., Part II. and the Staff Manual respectively. Title pages will be prepared in manuscript.

Hour, Date, Place	Summary of Events and Information	Remarks and references to Appendices
21-10-15 ANNEQUIN	In Billets - Physical drill before breakfast for all men, and N.C.Os on parade learning words of command, drill etc. In the afternoon - All platoons training in Grenade throwing etc.	AWB
22-10-15 " "	In Billets - do - do - Inspection of Clothing, equipment etc. of left half Battalion by C.O.	AWB
23-10-15 " "	In Billets - Parades as on 21-10-15. Inspection of clothing arms and equipment etc. of Right half Battalion by C.O.	AWB
24-10-15 " "	In Billets - Divine Service.	AWB

Army Form C. 2118.

WAR DIARY
~~INTELLIGENCE~~ SUMMARY

(Erase heading not required.)

Instructions regarding War Diaries and Intelligence Summaries are contained in F.S. Regs., Part II. and the Staff Manual respectively. Title pages will be prepared in manuscript.

Hour, Date, Place		Summary of Events and Information	Remarks and references to Appendices
25.10.15	ANNEQUIN	In Billets during morning.	AWB
"	CAMBRIN	In Trenches, 11. a.m. Relieved Cameronians.	AWB
26.10.15	"	In Trenches. One man killed. Wet weather. Reinforcement of 25 men joined (M.G. & Signallers)	AWB
27.10.15	"	In Trenches. Improving Trenches. Wet weather. — do —	AWB
28.10.15	"	In Trenches. — do — — do —	AWB
29.10.15	"	In Trenches during morning. 2 men wounded. Left Trenches and had a long march to GONNEHEM to new Billets.	AWB
30.10.15	"	In Billets. 540 men had a hot bath at Ecoles des Jeunes Filles, BETHUNE.	AWB

Army Form C. 2118.

WAR DIARY
or
INTELLIGENCE SUMMARY

(Erase heading not required.)

Instructions regarding War Diaries and Intelligence Summaries are contained in F. S. Regs., Part II. and the Staff Manual respectively. Title pages will be prepared in manuscript.

Hour, Date, Place	Summary of Events and Information	Remarks and references to Appendices
31.10.15. GONNEHEM In Billet.	Divine Service. Fitting Clothing, and inspection of Headquarters and Transport by C.O.	And
11.15		
	An Barker Lieut	
	Adj 7 A/S Highlanders	

19th Infantry Brigade.

2nd Division.

(Battn. transferred to
98th Bde. 33rd Div.
28.11.15)

WAR DIARY

2nd BATTN. THE ARGYLL & SUTHERLAND HIGHLANDERS.

N O V E M B E R

1 9 1 5

Attached:

Appendix A.

Army Form C. 2118.

WAR DIARY
or
INTELLIGENCE SUMMARY
(Erase heading not required.)

Instructions regarding War Diaries and Intelligence Summaries are contained in F. S. Regs., Part II. and the Staff Manual respectively. Title pages will be prepared in manuscript.

Hour, Date, Place	Summary of Events and Information	Remarks and references to Appendices
1.11.15. GONNEHEM.	In Billets. Physical Drill before Breakfast. Practicing Trench warfare. All officers Bomb Throwing Instruction.	
2.11.15. — do —	— do — Parades — do — — do — (Special Roman Catholic Service held, 9 a.m.)	
3.11.15. — do —	— do — Parades — do — — do — (Regimental Concert held 6.30. p.m.)	
4.11.15. — do —	— do — Parades as on 1st inst. —	
5.11.15. — do —	— do — Battalion Route March. Subalterns instruction in Bayonet Fighting in the afternoon, 2. p.m.	
6.11.15. — do —	— do — Physical drill before Breakfast. Company parades under Company Commanders.	

WAR DIARY or INTELLIGENCE SUMMARY

Army Form C. 2118.

(Erase heading not required.)

Hour, Date, Place	Summary of Events and Information	Remarks and references to Appendices
7.11.15. GONNEHEM.	In Billets, during morning, packing up.	
10.30 a.m. 7.11.15. Route	Marched from GONNEHEM to New Billets at Beuvry. Took over Billets from 1st Hertfordshire Regt.	
8.11.15. BEUVRY	In Billets. Physical drill before breakfast. Battalion on carrying fatigues. Major A.F.G. Hyslop. D.S.O. left the Battalion to take over temporary command of 1st Battalion, Argyll & Sutherland Highlanders. Major F.W. Stewart, Presbyterian Chaplain rejoined on this ddte from Hospital. 2nd Lieut. G.A.S. Thomson joined.	

Army Form C. 2118.

WAR DIARY
or
INTELLIGENCE SUMMARY

(Erase heading not required.)

Hour, Date, Place	Summary of Events and Information	Remarks and references to Appendices
9.11.15. BEUVRY. In Billets.	Physical Drill before breakfast & Drill parades under Company arrangements. Captain C.B. Purvis joined.	
10.11.15. BEUVRY. In Billets.	Parades as on 9th Inst. Temporary Captain P.G. Lyle proceeded to the United Kingdom, and struck off strength. Notification received that C-in-C. authorises the grant of one months furlough to United Kingdom to all N.C.O.s & men who extend their Service under Section 87 (3) A.R. and who have signed Army Form W.3125.	

WAR DIARY
or
INTELLIGENCE SUMMARY

(Erase heading not required.)

Army Form C. 2118.

Hour, Date, Place	Summary of Events and Information	Remarks and references to Appendices
11.11.15 BEUVRY	In Billets. Proceeded to take over Support trenches and billets from 2nd Royal Welch Fusiliers at 5.40 a.m. Order cancelled when Head of Battalion reached Cambrin. Returned to Billets at BEUVRY. Capt. F.B. Langlands Pres. Chaplain left Battn.	
12.11.15 BEUVRY	In Billets during morning.	
9.25 a.m. 12.11.15.	Marched to ANNIQUIN and took over Billets from 20 whom L.S.	
ANNIQUIN		
13.11.15. — do —	In Billets. Physical drill for all available N.C.O.s men before breakfast. Trench fatigues. 2nd Lieut. K. Rolfe proceeded to Rouen and took over Adjutantcy of the Camp there. Training.	

Army Form C. 2118.

WAR DIARY
or
INTELLIGENCE SUMMARY
(Erase heading not required.)

Instructions regarding War Diaries and Intelligence Summaries are contained in F. S. Regs., Part II. and the Staff Manual respectively. Title pages will be prepared in manuscript.

Hour, Date, Place		Summary of Events and Information	Remarks and references to Appendices
14.11.15.	ANNIQUIN	In Billets. Divine Service. French Fatigues.	
15.11.15.	— do —	In Billets. French Fatigues. 12 men attached to R.E. 251st Coy. (Tunnelling)	
16.11.15.	— do —	In Billets. French Fatigues	
17.11.15.	— do —	In Billets. — do —	
18.11.15.	— do —	In Billets during morning. Took over trenches from 1st Middlesex Regt. about 11. a.m., Relief carried out no casualties	
	CAMBRIN		

WAR DIARY or INTELLIGENCE SUMMARY

Army Form C. 2118.

(Erase heading not required.)

Hour, Date, Place	Summary of Events and Information	Remarks and references to Appendices
19.11.15. CAMBRIN In Trenches	Enemy prolific in the use of Hand grenades, rifle grenades and trench mortars. No Casualties.	
20.11.15. —do— In Trenches, —do— —do— —do—	No. 8593. Pte J. McKown & No. 10271 Pte S. just wounded, the latter returned to duty.	
21.11.15. —do— In Trenches.	Enemy using Hand Grenades, Rifle Grenades, trench mortars and shell fire. No. 6467. Pte D. Forsyth, wounded.	
22.11.15. —do— In Trenches (cont)	Mine blown up by the 180th Coy, R.E. between the trenches of the opposing troops about 30 yards from our fire trench. The Crater formed was occupied by Grenadiers and men of the	Appx. A

WAR DIARY
or
INTELLIGENCE SUMMARY

Army Form C. 2118.

Hour, Date, Place	Summary of Events and Information	Remarks and references to Appendices
22.11.15. CAMBRIN.	Trenches. of the Battalion, and held against (Contd) the enemy. Casualties:- Killed:- No. 7647, Pte D. Reid, No. 7595 Pte W. Chapman No. 11193 Pte W. Lewis, No. 7942 Pte E. Paterson No. 7681 Pte R. Bonner. Wounded:- No. 3319. S/Cpl. J. Fowler, No. 1736 Pte W. Taylor No. 2904 S/Cpl. W. Logan, No. 7792 Pte H. Harkins No. 11284 Pte J. McKellar, No. 7960 Pte A. McTavish No. 2904 L/Cpl. J. Gillespie, No. 11146 Pte J. Stewart No. 2848 Pte A. Aitchison, No. 8396 L/Cpl. J. Clark No. 3420 Pte D. Fraser, No. 9520 Pte W. Hay No. 10992 Pte J. Logan, No. 1846 S/C. J. Campbell No. 7336 Pte J. McCartney, No. 6614 Pte J. Davis. (Contd)	

Army Form C. 2118.

WAR DIARY
or
INTELLIGENCE SUMMARY
(Erase heading not required.)

Instructions regarding War Diaries and Intelligence Summaries are contained in F. S. Regs., Part II. and the Staff Manual respectively. Title pages will be prepared in manuscript.

Hour, Date, Place	Summary of Events and Information	Remarks and references to Appendices
22.11.15. CAMBRIN	In the Trenches - (Contd) Reference work done on this date. The General Officer Commanding 19th Infantry Brigade directed the Commanding Officer to express to the Battalion his appreciation of the good work done by it on the 22nd, in occupying the crater and so gallantly holding it until it was possible to consolidate it, and in repelling the German counter attack. No. 8119 Cpl R. Gibson & No. 7036 Pte D. Webster awarded D.C. medals for gallant conduct on this date. Hy. Lieut. & Q.M. Mr. J. Potter joined from 3rd Battalion for duty as Quartermaster.	

1247 W 3299 200,000 (E) 8/14 J.B.C. & A. Forms/C. 2118/11.

Army Form C. 2118.

WAR DIARY
INTELLIGENCE SUMMARY
(Erase heading not required.)

Hour, Date, Place.	Summary of Events and Information	Remarks and references to Appendices
23.11.15. CAMBRIN	In trenches during morning, removed from Trenches and marched to Bethune.	
" BETHUNE	In Billets night of 23rd Nov.	
24.11.15 "	In Billets during morning, marched to new Billets at Mt. BERENCHON.	
" Mt. BERENCHON.	In Billets.	
25.11.15 "	In Billets. Cleaning up. H.C. R.Q.M. Mr J.H. Clayton proceeded to Base en Route to Edinburgh to join 3rd Battalion.	
26.11.15 "	In Billets. Physical training, Company Drill Officers Grenade Practice, N.C.O's instruction parade.	

WAR DIARY
INTELLIGENCE SUMMARY
(Erase heading not required.)

Army Form C. 2118.

Hour, Date, Place	Summary of Events and Information	Remarks and references to Appendices
27.11.15, Mt BEUVRY	Physical Training, Company Training, Grenadier Training, Machine Gun Training, N.C.O. Instructions. Hot Baths for 770 men.	
28.11.15 " "	Divine Service.	
12.noon, 28.11.15 " "	Battalion transferred from 19th Infantry Brigade, 2nd Division to 98th Brigade, 33rd Division. 2nd Lieut. W.F.B. Shaw & 2nd Lieut. H.L. Calder joined.	
29.11.15 " "	Physical training before Breakfast. Battalion Route March, 10.a.m.	
28.11.15 " "	2nd Lieut. C.P. Stevenson joined. 2nd Lieut. R.P. Gardner joined.	

Army Form C. 2118.

WAR DIARY
or
INTELLIGENCE SUMMARY

(Erase heading not required.)

Instructions regarding War Diaries and Intelligence Summaries are contained in F. S. Regs., Part II. and the Staff Manual respectively. Title pages will be prepared in manuscript.

Hour, Date, Place	Summary of Events and Information	Remarks and references to Appendices
30.11.15. Mt BERENCHON	In Billets, during morning, removed to Billets at Le TOURET at 9.30 a.m.	
" — Le TOURET.	In Billets. Taking over new Billets.	

F. C. Lane
Lieut Colonel
Cmdg
Regt. of Arty; Futhr. High^{rs}

A P P E N D I X   "A"

Appy. A.

REPORT ON OPERATIONS ON MONDAY, 22nd. NOVR: 1915.

About 6.45 a.m. the 180th.Tunnelling Company exploded a counter mine to the South of the Etna Salient in G2 Z2 Section. The crater formed was situated about 30 yards from our fire trench between the crater known as the "ETNA CRATER" which is East and slightly North of the Salient, and the crater formed by the mine explosion at the commencement of the attack on the 25th.September,- After the explosion and under cover of the smoke, 10 grenadiers under command of Corporal Gibson, with water and rations, 5 spades and as many grenades as they could carry rushed across and occupied the crater. After the Grenadiers had got into the crater a message came back from Corporal Gibson asking for some duty men, 5 were sent out, about 5 minutes after another message came for more, ten more were sent in, this party lost 1 man killed and 2 men wounded crossing the open, both messages were brought by Pte. Webster who was fired at on each occasion, both coming and going. Returned with the last party. The crater was almost twice the size it was expected to be.

During the previous night a tunnel under the parapet had been commenced, and as soon as it was through a sap was begun, the party in the crater commenced sapping backwards. Communication with the crater was maintained by throwing messages across, and the supply of grenades was kept up in the same way. The party in the crater reported about 11.a.m. that they could hear the Germans digging towards them from the direction of their trenches grenades were thrown in the direction of the sounds; the party was harassed all day by rifle grenades fired from the direction of the crater formed by the Germans on the 11th.November, 1915. Several casualties occurred and both sapping and bombing was very difficult. About 3.30.p.m. a heavy mist came down and the wounded who could walk came out of the crater; the whole party was then relieved. Lieut. Moir organized the Bomb defence, and 2nd.Lieut.Maclaren with a working party the consolidating of the lip. A parados of sand bags was first commenced, but owing to the pulverized nature of the sides of the crater it was difficult to keep sandbags from slipping down, so support had to be given almost from the bottom of the crater which used an enormous amount of sandbags. Stores of grenades were formed all round the crater. The sap was completed about 4.30.p.m. About 5.p.m. hostile bombs began to fall into the crater in large quantities from three sides, the grenadiers replied and fire was opened from the parapet to cover the South Side of the Crater, hostile trench mortars and rifle grenades were also directed at the crater.

An arrangement had been made early in the day with the O.C., 47th.Field Howitzer Battery to fire over the Crater as near to it as he could when called on for support, which he now did, and the 17th.Battery also opened fire on the German trenches.

Some difficulty was experienced in keeping up the supply of grenades as those coming up from the Brigade Reserve Store had no detonators in them, grenadiers could not be spared to do this so the stretcher bearers were shown how to do it and did excellent work. The 6th.Trench Mortar Battery and the 19th.Brigade trench Mortars assisted by firing into the German craters where rifle grenade fire was coming from. The attack lasted about half an hour and then died down. Finding I could not replace casualties and afford relief to the Grenadiers without unduly weakening the Grenade Stations in the Section, I asked the O.C., 5th.Scottish Rifles to lend me 50 Grenadiers, which he did. The Grenadiers in the crater were then organized as a party of 15 in 4 hour reliefs, and a working party of 15 in same reliefs.

(contd)

2.

When it became quiet I asked the O.C., Sapping Platoon, 1st. Cameronians who was working in the trenches to take half a platoon into the crater and help consolidate, which he did with excellent results - By day light a parados of at least 4 feet high had been completed all round, head cover put up in places and the lip of the crater sandbagged all round, the sap also was improved and deepened,

During the attack an officer dressed in English uniform was in the sap shouting retire, he ceased on torrents of abuse being hurled at him by Lieut. Moir, he was not recognised; owing to things at the time being rather critical there was no time to take action. A strange officer shortly before the attack reported himself to me as having been sent to take over command of the Tunnelling Company and was directed to its Headquarters. Could this be inquired into as it is now thought this officer may have been a German Spy.

Total Casualties 5 Killed 16 Wounded
The crater was named Gibson's Crater

T. L. Gore   Lieutenant-Colonel,

23-11-15.   Commanding, 2nd. Argyll & Sutherland Highlanders.

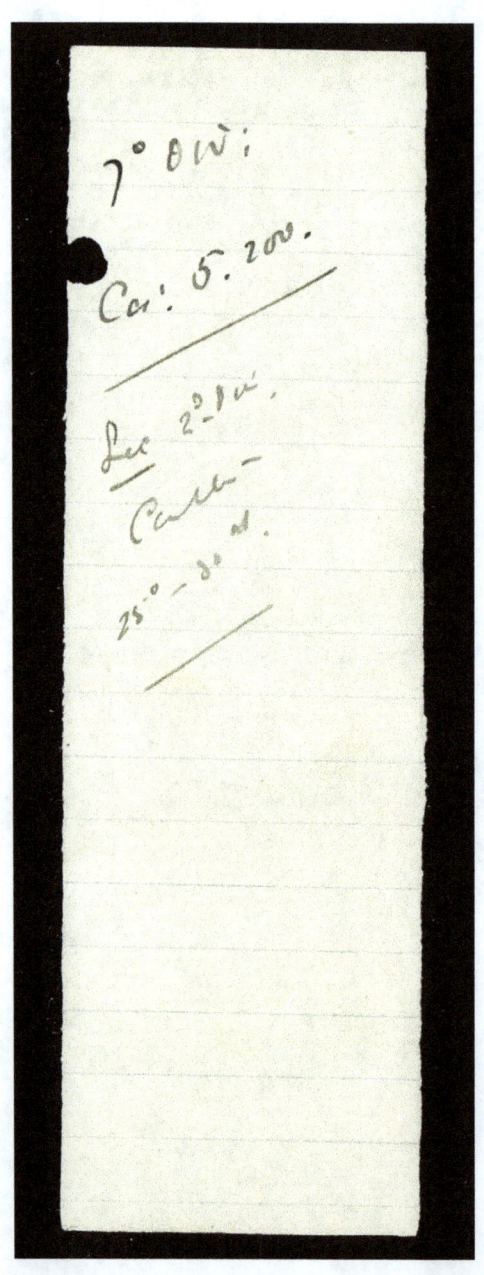

www.ingramcontent.com/pod-product-compliance
Lightning Source LLC
Chambersburg PA
CBHW080851230426
43662CB00013B/2076